Dear Mary, Dear Luther

A Courtship in Letters

JILL MARIE SNYDER

AuthorHouse™
1663 Liberty Drive
Bloomington, IN 47403
www.authorhouse.com
Phone: 1 (800) 839-8640

© 2015 Jill Marie Snyder. All rights reserved.

No part of this book may be reproduced, stored in a retrieval system, or transmitted by any means without the written permission of the author.

Published by AuthorHouse 05/27/2015

ISBN: 978-1-4969-6372-7 (sc)
ISBN: 978-1-4969-6373-4 (hc)
ISBN: 978-1-4969-6371-0 (e)

Library of Congress Control Number: 2015900549

Print information available on the last page.

Any people depicted in stock imagery provided by Thinkstock are models, and such images are being used for illustrative purposes only.
Certain stock imagery © Thinkstock.

This book is printed on acid-free paper.

Because of the dynamic nature of the Internet, any web addresses or links contained in this book may have changed since publication and may no longer be valid. The views expressed in this work are solely those of the author and do not necessarily reflect the views of the publisher, and the publisher hereby disclaims any responsibility for them.

Contents

Preface ix

Acknowledgements xiii

Before the Letters 1

The Letters 19

    1937 25

    1938 81

    1939 141

    1940 221

Mary and Luke 296

Epilogue 313

Sources 317

Census citations 321

Documents 325

For Mom, Dad, and Dale
I miss you every day....

Preface

My parents, Mary Brooks Snyder and Luther William Snyder, met sometime in late 1935 when they were paired in a wedding procession at the Bethel African Methodist Episcopal (AME) Church in Wilkes-Barre, Pennsylvania, where they lived. My father's aunt, Delaphine Snyder Haley, lived next door to my mother's family on North State Street in Wilkes-Barre. After that first meeting, my father would frequently visit his aunt for a few minutes, then wander over to my mother's front porch to spend hours chatting with her and her sister Sara. At first, they weren't sure which sister was the attraction, but over time, it became clear it was Mary.

In 1937, my father left Wilkes-Barre to work for the summer in Asbury Park, a resort town on the New Jersey shore. Mary and Luther began writing letters to each other, and their correspondence lasted for three and one-half years until they were married in January of 1941. During this period, they saw each other only a few weeks a year. Each saved their letters, leaving a nearly complete set of correspondence chronicling their romance.

I decided to publish the letters because my mother wanted to publish them. After marrying, my parents moved to New Haven, Connecticut. During the 1960s, they were acquainted with a young surgeon, Dr. Richard Selzer, not yet the well-known author he would later become. Knowing of his interest in writing, my mother told Dr. Selzer about

Preface

the love letters and she asked if he thought they could get published. As gently as he could, he told her no. She was very disappointed.

Mary died in 2007. A few years later, I began the project to transcribe the letters and fulfill her wish. The letters reveal the emotional track of Mary and Luther's courtship. Luther is the pursuer, always being honest with Mary about where she stands. Step-by-step he proclaims his feelings as he progresses from attraction to love. The media often portray African American males as brutes, lacking feelings and deep emotions. Luther's authentic expressions of romantic love will be a revelation for many. Mary—sassy, feisty and mercurial—is a very smart young lady. She continues to date others until Luther makes it clear she is the only one. She accepts his evolving emotional state, never pushing for a greater commitment than he's ready to make.

It is wonderful to witness my parents' burgeoning relationship. Gradually, their intimacy deepens until they reach a point when they both know they're ready to become man and wife.

I thought it important to give readers the full context for Mary and Luther's relationship, and for readers to understand how two African American families had arrived in Wilkes-Barre, a small coal city in northeastern Pennsylvania. Researching the Brooks and Snyder family histories led to the discovery of many stories about my ancestors that had not been passed down.

Now, I understand better my parent's emotional connection. Both were descended from African Americans who had likely escaped enslavement through the Underground Railroad. Both families had experienced acts of racism that had devastating consequences. Both of their mothers were outcasts in their respective communities: my maternal grandmother Stella because she was a white woman who had married an African American; my paternal grandmother Maude because she was an unwed mother at a time when it was much less accepted than it is today.

I no longer view Mary and Luther as a child views a parent. Now, I see their full humanity—their hopes and dreams, their disappointments. The converging forces of racism and economics made it impossible for them to fulfill their full potential so they poured their hopes into their children. For that, I am eternally grateful.

Acknowledgements

I want to thank my brother Roy and sister-in-law Iris for their support of this project. Roy didn't hesitate to give his consent to publish the letters and has encouraged me every step of the way. I'm also thankful for the encouragement of my cousins Karen Garcia and Barbara Qualls.

I feel deeply grateful for the wise advice of Stephen L. Carter and Enola Aird. I must express heartfelt gratitude to Dr. F. Kay Byron-Twyman, who proofread the letters early in the project. I'm also grateful for Noël Kristan Higgin's comforting counsel and for sharing her professional editorial skills.

Ancestry.com is a wonderful resource that started me on the trail of learning more about my ancestors. However, I must acknowledge the Columbia County Historical Society for their gracious and invaluable assistance in helping me compile a more complete story. I also want to thank the Luzerne County Historical Society.

Last, I owe a debt of gratitude to the late Emerson I. Moss for his book, *African Americans in the Wyoming Valley 1778-1990*. I was able to identify many Wilkes-Barre friends mentioned in the letters because of his book.

Before the Letters

Most of the Brooks and Snyder known family history took place in Pennsylvania. Pennsylvania is named after William Penn, a wealthy English Quaker. In 1681, he accepted a land grant to establish a province in British North America in exchange for a debt Britain's King Charles owed to Penn's father. Penn requested the grant because he believed that the province would be a haven for Quakers. Quakers, a religious sect, were often persecuted in England for their rejection of church rituals, their opposition to war, and their anti-slavery convictions.

Despite Quaker opposition, about four thousand slaves had been brought to Pennsylvania by 1730, most of them owned by English, Welsh, and Scotch-Irish colonists. The census of 1790 showed that the number of African Americans had increased to about ten thousand with the number of enslaved remaining between three and four thousand.

The Pennsylvania Gradual Abolition Act of 1780 was the first emancipation statute in the United States. Because the emancipation act allowed any enslaved person born in Pennsylvania to be free after twenty-eight years, Pennsylvania was regarded as a land of freedom for those who risked escape from enslavement in Southern states. Antebellum Pennsylvania was a hub for the escape routes from several geographic areas. Pennsylvania had an international port at Philadelphia that was a natural meeting place for boats traveling north from Virginia, Maryland, and Delaware. There was constant traffic at the port, including foreigners as well as indigenous Blacks. Thus, fugitives and their helpers could easily blend in with the other travelers.

Henry and Sara Jones

Much of the early history of my mother's family takes place in the tiny village of Catawissa, Columbia County, Pennsylvania. Nestled between a mountain ridge and the Susquehanna River, Catawissa was first settled by Quakers in the late 1700's. They built a log meeting house on a knoll a short distance from the meeting point of the Catawissa Creek and the north branch of the Susquehanna River. In the rear of the structure there is a hillside burial ground surrounded by a stone wall. Three generations of my family are buried there.

The earliest evidence of my family living in Pennsylvania is found in the 1850 census for Henry and Sara Jones and their children. The census shows the family living in Maine Township, not far from Catawissa, next to another Black family, Andrew and Mary Tarr and their seven children. Both Andrew and Henry's occupations are listed as "forgeman."

By 1860, Henry and Sara were living in Catawissa and had six children: Mary Margaret, my great-grandmother, plus Anna, Albert, Arthur, James, and Sara (called Sallie). Henry's occupation is listed as farm laborer.

Although little oral history was passed down to us about Henry and Sara, my mother often said her enslaved ancestors escaped the South because they feared being "sold down the river" to work on the cotton plantations in Mississippi and Louisiana. She believed that Henry and possibly Sara were aided by the Underground Railroad.

In the 1850 census, both Henry and Sara's birthplaces are listed as New York, which some in the family believe may be Sara's true birthplace. However, the 1860 census recorded their birthplace as Pennsylvania. This was a clue they may have been hiding their true origins, or at least Henry's. For their safety, it was necessary to hide the truth. The period of 1850 up to the Civil War was a dangerous time for escaped slaves due to the passage of the Fugitive Slave Act. Enacted by the United States Congress, this law gave slaveholders rights to organize a posse at any point in the United States to aid in recapturing slaves. Court and law enforcers everywhere in the United States were obligated to assist the slaveholders.

In Columbia County, many citizens sympathized with Southern slave owners. Paid slave catchers searched the county for fugitive slaves and to also kidnap free Blacks who had been residents of the county for years. Columbia County, possessing strong and active Black communities, was known for its militant resistance to slave hunters and kidnappers. This militancy led to deadly armed conflicts between the races. To find safety, many Blacks living in Columbia County fled to Canada.

Despite the dangers, Henry and Sara remained in Catawissa with their young family. Sadly, Sara died in 1860 before the Civil War and the Emancipation Proclamation, leaving Henry to care for his family alone.

Henry's obituary, published in the *Catawissa News Item* on Thursday, September 7, 1882, confirmed my mother's oral history:

> "Mr. Henry Jones (colored), who lives near this town, and who is widely known through-out this section of the country, died at his residence Tuesday afternoon last, of pleuro-pneumonia, after an illness of five days. The life of the deceased was an eventful one and would, if published, rival in interest the famed

"Uncle Tom's Cabin." He was born in slavery near Winchester, Virginia, in about 1807; after remaining a slave for about twenty years, he made his escape, aided by his master, and after a long and perilous journey through the mountains and swamps of Virginia and Maryland—traveling by night and hiding through the day—he reached McKinney's Iron Works, near Williamsport, where he remained for some time and then went to [New] York State where he was married, and thence to Mainville. About thirty five years ago he came to this place where he remained up to the time of his death. He was the father of seven children, six of whom are still living—three sons and three daughters. His wife died in 1860 in this place. "Old Henry," as he was familiarly called, was a favorite of everyone and his death is universally regretted."

I suspect Sara may have died in childbirth, and that one of her children died at birth since I have not found any record of a seventh child.

The Brooks Family

Henry and Sara's daughter, my great-grandmother Mary Margaret, married Clarence Augustus Brooks (sometimes called Augustus or Gus) of Baltimore, Maryland, on December 23, 1873, as noted in the records of the First Methodist Church of Catawissa.

It has been passed down through the family that Augustus had "two families" and often traveled back to Baltimore; however, no details were passed down to explain the meaning of this. It's possible that he may have been divorced or widowed before his marriage to Mary Margaret and had children in Baltimore that he would visit.

My mother always described Mary Margaret's oldest daughter Harriet, called Hattie, as "my father's half-sister." She was born November 16, 1866, seven years before Mary married. The identity of Hattie's father was a family secret that was never revealed. Because Hattie had a much lighter complexion than other members of the family, my mother suspected she was fathered by a white man.

The next oldest child, Irene, was born in 1872, also before Mary wed, and she also appeared to have a white father. My grandfather explained Hattie and Irene's light complexion to my mother by saying that Mary had two husbands, but there was never any explanation for who that other "husband" might be. It has the ring of an adult's explanation to a child to avoid telling the true story. I have not found any hint of another marriage, and it pains me to consider the possibility that Mary Margaret may have been a rape victim.

In addition to Hattie and Irene, the other children in the Brooks family were George, Theodore, Sara Jane, Charles, Grandis, and my grandfather, Clarence Augustus Brooks Jr., born in 1879.

My grandfather graduated from Catawissa High School in 1899. His diploma, which I still have, lists the subjects he studied:

> Arithmetic, Algebra, Plane Geometry, Natural Philosophy, Botany, Bookkeeping, Physiology, Orthography, Reading, English Grammar and American Literature, Rhetoric, General History, U.S. History, Civil Government, Political and Physical Geography, Latin Grammar, Caesar, Cicero, Chemistry and Moral Philosophy.

In the fall of 1899, he entered Howard University with the goal of becoming a doctor. Sadly, his father died December 17, 1900, of cancer and my grandfather was unable to continue his studies.

Before the Letters

My mother's letters reflect her father's protectiveness of his family. After learning the fate of his siblings, I understood his motivation.

Before my great-grandfather's death in 1900, the family had suffered the tragic death of Irene on October 17, 1895. Irene was married to John James, a native of nearby Bloomsburg. She tragically drowned fetching water to do laundry. The *Catawissa News Item* reported that she had gone to a friend's house near the town's wharf to do some washing, and took a couple of buckets to the canal to get some water. Her body was later found on the bottom of the canal. No one saw her enter the water but her death was ruled an accident.

Irene's husband John had been working in Connecticut for some time and was not believed to be in Catawissa when she died. However, rumors about the true cause of her demise swirled within the family for decades. Some suspected Irene's husband had sneaked into Catawissa and killed her; others believed she had committed suicide.

Irene was survived by a daughter, Lydia.

Sadly, my grandfather's brother Grant Brooks, only aged fourteen, died from tonsillitis in April of 1903. The next death in the family occurred thirteen years later, in August of 1916, with the gruesome demise of Theodore. He was a laborer and had found short-term work in Reading. When the work ended, he attempted to return home by hopping onto a freight train. The train was going too rapidly and he was unable to retain his hold, falling beneath the cars. His left leg was crushed from the hip down and he sustained internal injuries.

A year later, Charles died at the age of 31 after a long bout with tuberculosis. He had suffered his own grief, losing his only child, a five-month-old son, Grant, just six months before from pneumonia. Charles was described in his obituary as an "industrious young man and an employee of the All Wear Shoe Factory, and a member of the Catawissa M.E. Church."

On Monday, November 8, 1920, Mary Margaret, the stalwart matriarch of the Brooks family, died suddenly at her home, worn out from a lifetime of hard work and grief. She was seventy-six. Her *Catawissa News Item* obituary reads as follows:

> "Mrs. Brooks had been around the house during the afternoon. She complained of feeling tired and sat down. A few minutes later she was found dead. She was the daughter of Henry and Sara Jones of Mainville, and wife of Augustus Brooks who preceded her to the grave 20 years ago. She was a member of the Methodist Church and highly esteemed and well known. She is survived by two daughters, Mrs. J Frank Parks of Bloomsburg, Mrs. Wilbur Rux of town, and two sons, Gus and George Brooks, Williamsport, one brother, Arthur Jones, who made his home with her and two sisters. Sallie Jones, who also lived with her, and Mrs. Anna Jones of Williamsport, also survive as do 14 grandchildren and 4 great grandchildren.

George Brooks, my grandfather's last living brother, passed away in 1921, cause unknown, leaving just my grandfather Gus and his two sisters Hattie and [Sara] Jane remaining. Jane lived until 1936 when she lost her life to cancer at the age of fifty-nine.

My mother adored her Aunt Jane, describing her as having very high moral standards, eschewing alcohol, skirts above the knee, and nail polish. Jane was in the first graduating class of Bloomsburg High School and an active member of the Catawissa Methodist Church.

Clarence Augustus Brooks I

Mary Margaret Jones Brooks (center) with
daughters Irene (left) and Sara Jane (right).

The Paul Family

Mary and Charles Paul were my mother's maternal grandparents. Mary, born in 1875, was the daughter of William and Amelia Dietz Davis. William Davis was Welsh and had come to this country to work in the coal mines. Pennsylvania was a popular destination for Welsh immigrants, especially those who had worked in the coal mines, because they could apply the skills they had learned in their native country to jobs in Pennsylvania's coal region.

My mother always said that her grandmother Mary was born in Wales and brought to America as a baby but census records and her death certificate all indicate she was born in the U.S. It's possible that Mary never went through the naturalization process; thus, she needed to hide her true birthplace.

Charles Paul was born in 1870 in Port Carbon, Pennsylvania, to James Paul and Mary Phillips Paul. My mother was told that Charles Paul was a descendant of a German soldier who fought on the side of the British in the Revolutionary War. During the American Revolution, Germany was divided into over three hundred principalities. Many of these tiny countries supplied soldiers to the British army during the war. Most of the soldiers came from the German principality Hesse-Cassel. As a consequence, during the war and ever since, all of the Germans fighting with the British were lumped together and called Hessians.

King George III paid for the Hessians' services because he didn't have enough soldiers in his own army to supply the needs of his commanders in America. Most of the Hessians received no compensation for their services beyond their daily bread. It was the Prince of Hesse-Cassel, Frederick II who made out like a bandit in his dealings with George III. He sold the services of twelve thousand Hessians to the English and kept most of the money for himself.

In total, nearly thirty thousand German soldiers fought for the British in North America. Once here, they discovered a thriving German-American community of almost two-hundred thousand people. For many Hessians, the possibilities in this rich, new land were a great enticement to desertion—a fact that Americans worked hard to promote with promises of free land for Hessians willing to switch sides. An estimated five thousand Germans stayed in America after the Revolutionary War ended.

My great-grandfather Charles Paul worked as a boiler inspector for the Reading railroad. He was also a member of the *Knights of the Golden Eagle*, a fraternal organization founded in 1873. With rituals based on the Crusaders, it still has members in Pennsylvania.

Charles and Mary had six children: Sarah, Mary, Lillian, Charles Jr., and Harry, plus their youngest daughter, my grandmother, Stella May, born September 5, 1897. Sometime in the late 1890s, the Paul family moved next door to the Brooks family on Merceron Street in Catawissa.

My mother often told the story of the first time her father saw Stella:

> "When my mother was just two years old and my father was twenty, he saw her playing outside her house and declared, "You're beautiful! I'm going to marry you when you grow up."

My grandfather left Catawissa for many years and lived at various times in three different Pennsylvania towns: Scranton, Jamestown, and Williamsport. He worked as a professional musician, playing the violin in area orchestras. He eventually returned to Catawissa and on November 5, 1917, when Stella was just twenty and my grandfather was thirty-eight, they eloped to Scranton where they were married in a civil ceremony.

Stella was immediately rejected by her family. She saw her mother and sisters a few times during the ensuing years, but never saw or spoke to her father or brothers Charles Jr. and Harry again.

Stella and Gus remained in Scranton, living at 434 Lee Court. My mother, Mary Estelle, was born August 8, 1918, and my Aunt Sara Jane, Uncle Clarence Augustus Brooks III, and Aunt Lillian Irene quickly followed.

My mother recalled that Scranton's Black families were not allowed to live in homes facing the street. They were confined to living in dwellings that faced back alleys. To improve the family's circumstances, my grandfather moved the family to Bloomsburg when my mother was a little girl.

Bloomsburg is a lovely college town near Catawissa, also situated along the banks of the Susquehanna River. It had a small African American community since the 1800s. An article in the *Bloomsburg Daily Sentinel* from May 18, 1893, lists the names of several African American men who had started a baseball team, three of whom married into the Brooks family:

> "The colored boys have organized a Base Ball Club under the name of the Dillon Base Ball Club of Bloomsburg. It is composed of the following persons, John Banks, David Dooten, **John James**, Robert Hawkins, George West, Ed Green, William Johnson, W.E. Stuckey, **Frank Parks**, **Wilbur Rux**, Richard Reed and Chas. Stuckey."

My grandfather's half-sister Hattie was married to John Frank Parks (called Frank). Hattie and Frank had ten children: Bishop, James, John Frank Jr., Charles, Mary Catherine, Amanda, Margaret, Harriet, Sara Jane, and Helen. With the age difference between Hattie and my grandfather, and his marriage at a relatively late age, my mother's Parks cousins were adults or reaching adulthood by the time my mother was born. Her cousin Helen was a great source of pride for the whole Parks and Brooks clan because she was the first in the family to attend college. When my mother was a child, Helen lived in Alabama and taught English at Tuskegee Institute.

Frank Parks was a barber, and my grandfather Gus trained with Parks for a while when he was young, after dropping out of Howard University when his father died. In the late 1920s, Gus moved his young family to Bloomsburg to rejoin Frank's barber shop at 228 Center Street. The two men built a prosperous business, servicing a mostly white clientele.

Mary remembered her youth in Bloomsburg as both a joyful time and a painful time. Her most cherished memory was the Sunday afternoon music performances in the family living room:

> "My father taught me to play the piano and Sara to play the violin. On Sunday afternoons, after dinner, we would invite family and friends to come by and have musicales in the living room. Me, Sara and my father would play together. Everyone looked forward to those afternoons."

Mary also recalled her family being terrorized:

> "Men in white robes burned crosses on our lawn because my father was married to a white woman. Then one day the barber shop was set on fire and burned to the ground. My parents were sure the same men were the arsonists. My mother always believed that it was her own brothers who were the ringleaders."

After this incident, concerned about the family's safety, my grandfather left Bloomsburg and moved the family to Wilkes-Barre. Frank Parks remained in Bloomsburg. He rebuilt his business at a new location but became increasingly abusive toward Hattie and their ten children, leading to a horrific tragedy that still overshadows our family.

The new Brooks residence in Wilkes-Barre was at 17 North State Street, next door to the family of Delaphine Snyder Haley, my father's aunt.

The Snyder Family

On my father's side, the earliest record of the Snyder family is in the 1860 census in the township of Hegins, today located within the Pottsville Metropolitan Area of Schuylkill County, in the coal region of east central Pennsylvania.

The area has a rich ethnic heritage. People came to Schuylkill County from all over Europe—Ireland, Germany, Italy, Slovakia, Lithuania, and Russia—to work the mines and farm the fields.

In 1860, there was a small enclave of Blacks families living in the area including the Britton, Jones, Enty and Tarr families. The enclave also included my paternal great-great-grandparents, Simon and Julia Snyder. Some may have arrived in the Pottsville area as escaped slaves. The Underground Railroad ran through Pottsville. The red brick house at 622 Mahantango Street is a documented station. It was once owned by Quaker James Gillingham.

Simon and Julia had a son, Simon Jr., born about 1853. In addition to Simon Jr., there were two daughters: Elizabeth, Henrietta (called Harriet), and two children they may have taken in as foster children: Catherine Enty and Mary Ann Crapp. By 1880, Simon Sr. was no longer living but Julia was still in Pottsville, residing with her daughter Harriet who by then was married to James Fisher.

Simon Jr. married Charlotte Britton, born about 1856 to Daniel and Mary Britton. I found Mary's death certificate, recording that she suddenly died in 1913 of "apoplexy." The certificate also states she was born in Virginia in 1844 but her parents were unknown. Her birth date was likely earlier than 1844. It's possible she had escaped from enslavement in Virginia and didn't know her true birth date.

Simon Jr. and Charlotte made their home in Wilkes-Barre, Luzerne County, Pennsylvania. Like Bloomsburg and Catawissa, Wilkes-Barre is located along the Susquehanna River, but unlike those towns, it's a gritty industrial city. In the late 1800s and early 1900s, it was a prosperous area due to the anthracite coal mines. Anthracite coal is very hard, slow-burning, and smokeless, which made it ideal for home heating fuel. Unfortunately for the area's workers, the use of coal went into decline after World War I, replaced by oil and natural gas. Consequently, Wilkes-Barre's economy also suffered and it has never returned to the level of prosperity it previously enjoyed.

Simon and Charlotte benefited from Wilkes-Barre's turn-of-the-century prosperity. Simon began a career in the restaurant industry as a waiter when he was still a teenager. After his death on April 27, 1914, his obituary published in the Wilkes-Barre Record two days later shed light on his highly successful career as a chef:

> "The many friends throughout Wyoming Valley of Simon Snyder, one of Wilkes-Barre's best known colored residents, will be sorry to learn of his death, which occurred Monday night at his home at 233 Lincoln Street, of complications after a long ailment. He was aged about seventy-five and had resided in Wilkes-Barre the past thirty-five years, coming from Pottsville, where he was born, with the late John R. Kennedy, who

for many years was Wilkes-Barre's leading caterer and restaurateur.

He was one of the most experienced chefs in this part of the State and during his life prepared feasts for some of the most prominent men of the country, as well as for local people. He was in the employ of Mr. Kennedy until the latter's death and then entered the employ of the late M.Z. Charles and later went with John A. Redington, with whom he remained for a number of years. He was also employed at all of the principal hotels and restaurants of this city and vicinity and had a wide acquaintance with the traveling salesmen. He was always courteous, pleasant and happy and had a good word for all. Owing to his coming in contact with so many people he became quite a linguist and talked German and Italian."

Simon and Charlotte were the parents of nine children including seven sons and two daughters: Daniel, Harry, Harvey, Paul, Milton, Sylvester, Roy, my grandmother Maude and her sister Delaphine. My father, Luther William, was born January 30, 1911, to unwed Maude. Maude never revealed to my father the identity of his father. At the time, being an unwed mother brought a great deal of shame to both mother and child. Because he was fatherless, the immigrant children in his neighborhood taunted and bullied him, leaving him with a deep-seated sense of shame that he never overcame.

Maude as a young woman.

Luther (right) and friends, circa late 1920s.

My father's Aunt Delaphine was married to Edward Haley and they ran a boardinghouse out of their home at 15 North State Street. When my mother's family left Bloomsburg after the fire, they moved next door to the Haley family. My grandmother Stella and Mrs. Haley (as she was called by everyone) became close friends. The oral history I have about the Snyder family is mostly from the stories my mother told me.

Delaphine Haley had eight children: seven sons and one daughter, Emily. At the time the letters were written, Emily lived in Harlem with her husband Thomas Busch. Paul, known as Sunshine Haley, was an entertainer in his youth. These were the only two Snyder relatives I ever met, but the Snyder family story I remember most vividly is that of Emily and Paul's brother, David Haley.

David married young, and he and his wife had a baby boy, David Jr., who everyone called Sonny. David's wife was diagnosed with tuberculosis soon after Sonny's birth. David tried to find a sanitarium that would accept his wife, but all refused to admit a "colored" woman. In desperation, the family found a hospital in Canada that would admit her, but she died on the train in David's arms before reaching the hospital. David became so despondent he was admitted to the Retreat Mental Hospital, a state-run facility for indigent mental patients. His sister Emily took custody of Sonny.

The Letters

As I transcribed these letters, I had to decipher illegible words and names. Often by reading ahead to the response, I discerned the meaning of something in a previous letter.

My parents were both high school graduates with excellent command of English. However, there are numerous times when their concentration was focused on expressing emotion and not on spelling or formal grammar rules. These letters were often written hastily, and you'll notice now and then quirky phrasing, incomplete sentences, missing punctuation, and odd spellings. For example, my mother uses nite for night. My father often writes two words now commonly combined as one word such as *day light* and *for ever*. To preserve the authenticity of the letters, I made very few corrections.

You'll also notice that my father signs his letters Luke, often with quotation marks. For an unexplained reason, my mother always uses Luther in her salutation. When my father's letters were written on hotel stationery, I included the hotel's name and address. Unfortunately, a few of his 1939 letters are missing.

The Letters

Who's Who

My parents shared news about many of their friends in the letters, so I've included a "Who's Who" to give the reader a sense of their community. The information is based on census records, my own recollections of stories my mother told me, and Emerson Moss's work *African Americans in Wyoming Valley, 1778-1990.* My father was an avid tennis player, so many of his friendships were formed as a member of the South Side 'Y' tennis team.

Rudy Andruz—Owner of a 1929 Packard, he was a high school friend of my mother. Rudy was a native of St. Thomas, Virgin Islands.

Harry Paul Brown—The youngest son of a long-time Wilkes-Barre family, he was a boyfriend of my mother's youngest sister, Lillian. His father fought in both the Spanish-American War and World War I, and owned a trucking business called the Wyoming Valley Transfer Company. Harry's older sisters, Helen, Evelyn "Evie," Lois, and Georgia are also mentioned.

Emily Haley Busch—My father's first cousin who was married to Thomas Busch. During the 1930s and '40s, Mr. Busch was the building manager for 409 Edgecombe Avenue in Harlem. At the time these letters were written, 409 Edgecombe was becoming a desirable address for New York's African American cultural and political elite

Mary Buster—A high school friend of my mother's, she's often referred to as Mary B. Her mother, Georgia, was married to Griffen Reynolds, Mary's stepfather.

Louise Downey—My mother's closest friend in high school, she was the youngest child in a large family of nine children. In addition to her

Dear Mary, Dear Luther

brothers, she also had several sisters who are occasionally mentioned: Helen, Mildred, Rosabelle, Catherine, Bertha, and Alice.

Charles "Charlie" and Washington "Wash" Downey—Two friends of my father and older brothers of Louise Downey. "Wash" was a member of the Coughlin High School football team and captain of the 1930 track team.

Clarence Fisher—The son of Elmer and Besse Fisher and my father's second cousin. Elmer was adopted by my father's great-aunt Harriet (Simon Sr.'s sister) and her husband James.

John Foster—A friend of my mother's sister Sara.

William and Leroy "Buddy" Grimes—Brothers who were Wilkes-Barre friends of both my parents. Buddy was a porter at the Redington Hotel where my Uncle Clarence worked and my father had worked before leaving Wilkes-Barre.

Paul Haley—My father's first cousin, son of Delaphine and Edward Haley, he was an entertainer and dancer known as "Sunshine" Haley.

David Haley Jr. (Sometimes called "Davey" or "Sonny")—Son of my father's first cousin David and beloved nephew of Emily Haley Busch.

Beville Highsmith—A Wilkes-Barre acquaintance whose parents, Luther and Elizabeth Highsmith, were from North Carolina.

Christopher "Chris" and George Hillman—Wilkes-Barre friends of my parents, both tennis players with the South Side 'Y' tennis team.

Jerome "Brud" Holland—An All-American football player at Cornell University who frequently visited Wilkes-Barre.

Benjamin "Ben" Johnson—A native of the Luzerne County town of Plymouth, he visited Wilkes-Barre several times, often with his friend Andy MacDonald. Ben was a renowned sprinter on the Columbia University track team and set world records in 1935 and 1938. Due to a pulled muscle, he was unable to compete against Jesse Owens in the 1936 Olympics.

Hayward "Champ" Lambert—He and his wife were close friends of my father in Harlem's Sugar Hill neighborhood.

Andrew "Andy" MacDonald—A football player and baseball player for Wilkes-Barre's Myers High School, he was attending Lincoln University at the time the letters were written.

Verne McLoe—An amateur boxer.

Olin and Blanche Morris—Friends of my parents, Olin was another member of the South Side 'Y' Tennis team.

Harriet Oliver—An acquaintance of my parents, she left Wilkes-Barre for New York City to pursue dancing.

Harold and Edgar Patience—They were Wilkes-Barre brothers who were well known for their use of coal for novelties and sculptures. Their grandfather, Crowder Pacien, was a former slave who was owned by a Frenchman in the French West Indies. He fought in the Civil War as a soldier in the 103rd Infantry Regiment from Pennsylvania. Harold also played on the South Side 'Y' tennis team.

Evelyn Payne—A school friend of my mother who grew up in a large multigenerational household with her grandparents.

Howard "Doc" Reid—Another of my father's tennis buddies, he was the stepbrother of Dorothy Walker.

Maude Roach—A high school friend of my mother, her parents were from British Guiana. Her siblings Florence (Flossie), Milton, and Edgar are also mentioned.

Griffin "Griff" Reynolds—A porter in the Hotel Redington who was married to Georgia, Mary Buster's mother.

Arthur "Art" Sands—A friend of my parents, son of James and Amy Sands of Alabama. He had a sister, Louise, who is also mentioned.

Dorothy Walker—One of my mother's Scranton friends.

Johnny and Jocelyn Winfield—My father's closest friends in New York. He stayed with the Winfield's during the first few months he lived there.

1937

My parents' letters begin during the Great Depression. The Depression worsened the already harsh economic situation facing African Americans. They were the first fired and the last hired, suffering from an unemployment rate two to three times that of whites. In early public assistance programs, African Americans often received less aid than whites. Even some community organizations refused to serve Blacks.

In the face of these challenges, the best work my father could find after high school was as a hotel porter at Wilkes-Barre's Redington Hotel. The letters begin when he decided to leave Wilkes-Barre for the summer to work in Asbury Park, New Jersey. For my father, Asbury Park was a whole new, exciting world.

My mother was about to graduate from Coughlin High School, a milestone on her journey to adulthood. She was held back in an early grade due to a childhood illness that forced her to miss school for a lengthy period; thus, she was already eighteen. As a result of being held back, she and my Aunt Sara, one year younger, were in the same grade together for most of their schooling and graduated together.

In her early letters, my mother strained to sound mature in her responses to my father, but her youthfulness is evident.

The Letters

The members of the S.S.S (South Side Sisters) were my mother's high school girlfriends who spent after-school hours at the Wilkes-Barre South Side 'Y'. They organized parties and other social events. The South Side 'Y', formally called the Colored Young Men's Christian Association, was formed in 1922 when African Americans were refused membership to the established Y.M.C.A.

"Boo-Hoo" performed by Guy Lombardo and his Royal Canadians, was a popular song in 1937. According to the Canadian Songwriters Hall of Fame website, it reached number one on the U.S. charts.

May 27, 1937
Dear Mary,

I'm as sure as the sun shines that you are as sweet as when I left. Gee, it's swell down here but it would be perfect if you were here, you know I can't lose that longing for you. You better not let Sara see this letter because she might embarrass you some time—although I know you blush beautifully.

I went to a dozen hotels before I got a job. I like this hotel and I stay right here at the hotel.

I hope you answer this letter before Christmas 1947, because I'll be anxious to hear from you.

There are plenty of places to go down here but I'm too busy to go. Gee I'm always busy I can't help it.

Tell your Mother and Dad I said hello. Also Helen, Louise and her Mammy. I'm quite generous with my hello's, big shot. A nice juicy Boo-Hoo for the S.S.S. Club.

Always thinking of you.

"Luke"

Mr. Luther Snyder
c/o Hotel Alameda
207 Seventh Ave.
Asbury Park, N. J.

Wilkes-Barre, Pa
June 1, 1937
Dear Luke,

I loved reading your letter and you were sweet to write so promptly. You can't imagine how much I've missed you.

You were lucky to get a job so quickly even if you had to go to all those hotels. Have you been around much or are you still too busy?

There has been something doing here every night since you've been gone. On Thursday night Louise Downey had a birthday party. I had loads of fun although I missed you all the while I was there. Our dance was a big success, that is as big a success as you could expect at the "Y" since it had to end at 12:00.

We had company over the week-end from Friday until Monday night. Chris took us for that long-promised ride on Sunday. There were three girls and Chris, but we had loads of fun. I am trying to decide whether to go to that party tonight or not. Our exams start tomorrow so I really ought to rest tonight or I might be sleeping during the test.

Supper is ready so I will have to stop even if it is selfish. No more boo-hooing for the "SSS." We have 15 cents in our treasury now. We'll soon be going places.
Mary

The girls all say "hello"

(Additional note) You Darling! This is just a note to say that I just received your candy and I love it. Sara says that she and Brother enjoy it very much. But not so much as I do. Thanks loads.

Mary as a third-grader.

Sara (left) and Mary (right) embracing their friend Louise Downey.

Miss Mary Brooks
17 N. State Street
Wilkes–Barre, Pa.

Asbury Park
June 4, 1937
Dear Mary,

It was really swell to receive a letter from you—I only read it seventeen times since I received it. I don't start work steady until about the twentieth, except for week-ends, so until then I am vacationing. Every day, I put my dark glasses on and stroll up and down the boardwalk. Everyone wears dark glasses therefore everyone looks alike—White and colored.

It's lots of fun watching the waves roll in and out from the shore. I was walking down the beach and I saw a lady undressing so I didn't know whether to run and tell her she wasn't in her room or turn my head but before I could decide what to do she had her dress off but she had a bathing suit on, was I mortified.

I sit and watch the liners pass at night and in the daytime it's very picturesque. All you do is whistle and the fish just run to you. The first day I was there I almost whistled all the fish out of the sea—they had to stop me.

You can buy anything you want on the boardwalk. So big shots come down here to buy their fashions. I wish you could see the darn fool fang dangles they wear such as hats with no tops and just the sole of the shoe but it is the style.

Everywhere you go they have music in the barbershops, grocery stores, restaurants, on the boardwalk, at the dog show, in the park and where ever you enter. Every time I pass the merry-go-round it's playing

Boo-Hoo—it reminds me of the S.S.S. because they go around it in circles.

I took my shirts to a chinkie laundry and lost my ticket. You can imagine what he said when I went for them, the old foreigner.

I was to a dance Sunday night. It was pretty swell. I missed my dance with you though. I hope you make out in your exams. Here's luck to you.

It was nice of Chris to take you for a ride. George Hillman, Doc Reid and another fellow were down here Wednesday—I showed them the city.

Well Mary, regardless of where I go, what I see or what I do, I've all ways got pleasant memories of you, of our being together. Please don't forget me.

"Luke"

Asbury Park
June 4, 1937

Dear Mary:
It was really swell to recieve a letter from you, I only read it seventeen times since I recieved it.
I don't start to work steady until about the twentieth, except for week ends, so until then I am vacationing.

Dear Mary, Dear Luther

The Cadvocates was an informal club comprised of my father's buddies. Like the S.S.S., they organized parties and dances. This letter appears to be dated incorrectly. It was postmarked June 10th.

Wilkes-Barre, Pa
June 4, 1937

Dear Luther,

That was a very lovely letter and I certainly did enjoy reading it. If you keep on that way your name will go down in history. Napoleon was famous for his letters to Josephine while he was at Waterloo.

You certainly can be glad you aren't here now. It is so hot that one can scarcely get one's breath. If we whistled for fish in one of the streams around here we would probably get boiled fish.

Well, Mr. Cadvocate, your club's farewell party turned into a wake. Everyone came away mourning the fact that they even bothered to go to it. A sister S.S.S. was there and she gave the rest of our society a good description of a very sad affair. Sara and I weren't there, that was what was wrong with it.

Well, our exams are all over. You sent your good wishes a little too late. I flunked physics. The rest of the tests were O.K., thank heavens.

Luther, when you go strolling down the boardwalk won't you please keep your dark glasses on, especially when ladies haven't anywhere to disrobe. You surprise me with your boyish modesty. I thought that went out with red flannels.

We are going to the G.A.R. Prom on Tuesday night. Now I will give your alma mater a good once over to see what a really poor school looks like. Meyers and Coughlin are having a combined prom on Wednesday. There is a big crowd of kids going. It ought to be pretty nice. I hope so anyway.*

Luther, you ought to see Mary and Wash. They're going from worse to worser. On Saturday night Mary, Wash, John (Sara's John), Andy and Art were sitting on our front porch and Wash couldn't do a thing but kiss Mary. Sara & John ran a close second. Andy, Art and I had to just sit and look on. It's terrible how immodest people can be.

Goodness Luther, I know you are tired reading. My handwriting would tire anyone even me if I had to read it myself.

I've just heard a new song "Hold Me Tight, Hold Me Close, Hold Me Near." Somehow it reminds me of you. But then everything reminds me of you.

Mary

G.A.R, Meyers and Coughlin are Wilkes-Barre's high schools.

Father Divine was an African American spiritual leader from about 1907 until his death in 1965. His full self-given name was Reverend Major Jealous Divine, and he was also known as "the Messenger" early in his life. He founded the International Peace Mission movement. Its heyday was in the Depression years of the 1930s when it made headlines for its stance on racial integration. It was also known for its low-budget businesses in communities throughout New York and New Jersey. My father mistakenly spells his name 'Devine'.

June 11, 1937

Dear Mary,

Your missive was received with appreciation. Listen Mary, I'm not trying to make history. I'm trying to make love!

I'm getting awful colored being in the sun. I spend practically all day out of doors. It has been very warm here too but it turns cool at night.

I worked at a parking lot parking cars last week-end and the same man that hired me had a hot dog stand nearby. He got very busy so he asked me if I could make sandwiches and I told him that back home they call me "Sandwich Snyder." I'm always in the middle. Did I make some sandwiches!

There are several boys and girls from all over down here. They seem to be very congenial. We have lots of fun. But in the midst of my fun and hilarity I become despondent—well, that's you in me. A laugh really isn't appreciated unless it's with you.

One boy, a Georgian wants me to go back to his home in September. Another from Florida said I should go down there and work and still another from Washington D.C. is planning on going to California after Labor Day. So I have lots of offers to go several places but W – B first.

Father Devine has a barber shop and restaurant down here. You can get a haircut for ten cents, a shave for five cents, and a full course meal for fifteen cents. They also have "Peace" taxis and "Peace" ice for sale.

My modesty seems to have vanished. I saw some girls riding bikes on the board walk and it didn't faze me. Women never did bother me anyway—much.

The boardwalk is three and a half miles long. How would you like to sweep it off every day? By the time you would get to one end it would be the next day then you would have to start all over again. I only live one block from the ocean. I get up early in the morning about eleven thirty and inhale the sea breeze—it's great.

Well I suppose you can't fault Wash or Mary because everyone gets that way in life. If I were there I would be kissing you. I wouldn't mind.

Sorry to hear the farewell party was a flop but they can blame you and Sara—see you shouldn't do that.

Please take care and be in your dignity when you attend the G.A.R. Prom. You wouldn't have to be so careful when you attend the others. I hope you and all the others that attend have the swellest time possible. Please have a dance for me.

Tell me about it when you write next time.

I didn't know Andy was in town—tell him I said hello. Also a cheerio to your father, mother, sisters and brother.

I never grow tired of reading your handwriting but the reading of this letter should disgust you.

I'm ashamed of you flunking Physics. It's such an easy subject.

Well I also heard a new number and if you haven't heard it yet please do so—it's swell, the name of it is "The One Rose." Please answer soon—your letters are a consolation to me. One who is grateful to you always,

"Luke"

Wilkes-Barre, Pa.
June 17, 1937
Dear Luke,

Or would you rather "Sandwich Snyder." I'm always willing to oblige.

Goodness, we've been so busy that Sara thinks she's getting married. She keeps saying her wedding when she means graduation. I don't know whether I'm coming or going. Today was class day. We had a swell program this morning. Sara got a drum for class day gift because she is so quiet and maybe we will hear her now.

I received a bunch of lolly-pops to remind me of a bell-hop who is sweet enough to eat.

A couple of girls saw you and I together one night going over to the hotel when you had your uniform on. Sara told them who you were, hence the class gift.

Mary Buster's mother had her tonsils out on Tuesday and Mary has been the nurse. It's a wonder her poor mother isn't dead.

Edgar Patience got married to a girl from Philadelphia. Louise Downey and Alec Johnson are engaged. The love-bug sure is busy around here.

Ben Johnson was here. He took us all riding, showed us a few new dance steps and bought nearly all the ice cream Russell's had. Now he's sending Sara post-cards. She's going to put them in a scrap book when she gets one and if she gets one.

I haven't been over to the hotel for three weeks.* Yesterday, Mrs. Brown came to me and said that Helen Louise was hungry for me. Didn't think I tasted so good. The skinny Helen that runs the elevator sends her regards. So does the nice clerk—the one you don't like. So you see you still are somewhat of a big shot around there. Mr. Davies drew a picture of you. Kind of cute.

Luther, don't pay any attention to those boys. Pretty soon they'll be driving you wanderlust, and that will never do.

Answer real soon.

Mary

"37"

*Hotel Redington

Mary's high school graduation photo.

Asbury Park
June 21, 37
Dear Mary,

I'm sure you and Sara had a hectic past week but were well paid Friday night. Congratulations to you both for the presents—will send something later.

I attended the Asbury High commencement Friday. It was short and sweet. All the graduates wore grey caps and robes. Each girl carried a bouquet of roses and carnations. There were about thirty colored out of a class of 200. The exercises were held at the Convention Hall. They received their diplomas in a folder. There was a dance for the colored grads after also.

Ask Jimmy (Mary Buster), if there is any news. Tell her to take care of her mother also. Hello to Griff.

What do you think of your class day gift? Sara is very proper sometimes.

Everybody is doing. That bug sure will find you when it wants to. Luck to Edgar. Louise is out of your class now. I suppose when I return I'll find a lot of old married folks there.

I suppose Ben showed you some of the crazy steps they do down here, they are terrific. Tell skinny Helen and the nice clerk I return their regards cheerfully. So Davies is drawing funny pictures of me. Has he put them in the comics yet?

I showed a couple of fellows the pictures we took over to the park that Sunday. They say you and Sara are swell. They wanted your address so he could tell you I would be in good company if I went to Florida with him. I told him my girl wouldn't let me go. When the season closes down here I'm telling the engine man to put two extra engines on the train that I catch and puff and blow me home to you. I'm "Hatin' this Waitin' for you."

The Letters

 I hope you have a swell time tonight. I'm sure you'll look sweet and charming you know, "They Can't Take That Away from Me." Set one dance out and call it mine. I sure wish I were there to have it though. Tell all the girls tonight to dance or sit one for me.
"Luke"

My grandparents were close friends with Grace and Roger Tyler of Scranton. My mother and her siblings referred to them as Aunt Grace and Uncle Roger. The Tyler's had a brood of seven children and the two families often visited each other, sometimes for extended periods. However, they are rarely mentioned by name.

17 N. State Street
Wilkes-Barre, Pa.
June 25, 1937
Dear Luke,

I never had so much trouble writing a letter in my life. Every time I start somebody comes. This town is so beat that everyone is running around in circles trying to find something to do. There are only a few of us here and we seem to be stepping on each other's toes.

The Tonk's dance was sort of a disappointment. There were five girls to every one boy. We danced most of the dances with our escorts. Since my escort wasn't you I was bored to death. The second half was a little better because most of the stag girls had gone home and there was a more even number. I do wish you had been there, though.

Mildred Simpson had a party with a special orchestra for us to dance by. I don't know whose orchestra it was but it sounded sort of like it was related to our famous "Colonials." We had loads of fun anyway.

My mother and Sister have gone to Scranton for the week-end. Sara and Brother and I are keeping house. You would be surprised how domestic our Brother really is and you should see him clean fish. It really is a work of art the way he cuts them up. You wouldn't recognize them.

Mary B. spent the night with us. I mean I spent the night trying to get a stocking cap on her small head. My muscles were considerably harder this morning, thanks to Mary.

Luther, will you please tell that Florida pest that I really think that the Florida climate wouldn't agree with you and that Wilkes-Barre needs her good citizen and I need you.

If he insists on you going with him tell him to stop by and see me. I'll attend to him. Don't forget to have an extra engine put on that train because I am impatient.

Mary

Jimmy Lunceford, a band leader and saxophone player, was at the peak of his fame in 1937. Before performing professionally, he studied music at Fisk University and the City College of New York.

Asbury Park
June 29, 1937
Dear Mary,

It was nice hearing from you after the long suspense. Since you are a lady of leisure you should have lots of time for sleep.

Sorry to hear the Tonk's dance wasn't a large success, better luck next time. I deeply regret my absence and most of all, my dance with you.

Jimmy Lunceford is playing down here on the 5th. It seems to be the talk of the town. Tell some of the boys—they may be crazy enough to come down here.

Tell Mary B. to keep her nose clean. The fellow from Florida still insists that I go with him but I just let him rave on. As much as I want to go, my anxiety to see you surpasses the trip to Fla. I've been away about a month but it seems like three years.

Tell Sara the Florida boy is coming to W-B to see her. As I told you I showed him the pictures we took that Sunday.

Talk about shape, there are all types promenading up and down the boardwalk but I sure would like to gaze at yours again. Keep trim until I return. And write <u>soon</u>.
"Luke"

The Letters

Wilkes-Barre, Pa
July 6, 1937
Dear Luke,

    I received your missive with pleasure and although it was short it was sweet.

    I know you have had a delightful week-end. Ours wasn't bad. We had about twenty people at our house for two days. On Saturday night we had a jump up at Mary B.'s and on Sunday we were everywhere. Yesterday fifteen of us rented bikes over in Kingston. It was the first time I, or any of the girls for that matter, had ever ridden a bike. The boys are still ranking on us, but our spirits aren't daunted.

    Emily Haley came home and brought Dave's baby with her. The Snyder's have been congregated on the front and back porch ever since. Wait until you bring your family home. They'll even have the band playing the old song "Freckle-face." Maybe they'll change it to "Little Freckle Face."

    How did you enjoy the dance with Jimmy Lunceford? I know you forgot to sit one out for me, but I'll excuse you this time, because you're too far away to do anything else.

    Your friend Wash and Mary haven't been getting on so well since he came back. His other lady has sort of put a damper on their affair! Mary is broken-hearted, she says she is going to do something about it. But that won't be much. She and Sara are having a sort of silent battle over Andy MacDonald. He's in Philadelphia so maybe that will end that. Here's hoping.

    I guess I'll have to stop and rub my aches and pains. Bicycling done it. Hard old bikes. But I'd get used to it or else.

    Don't wait until Labor Day to answer
Mary

Asbury Park
7-10-37
Dear Mary,

Yours was received and enjoyed as usual.

Knowing that you and your friends enjoyed a pleasant week-end makes mine a success. This hotel looked like a 'frat house' because some girls from the Club Newark had a week-end here. They were draped all over the porch, banister and steps. We have an orchestra here at the hotel now and they dance on the porch in the evening. This is a very pretty place although it isn't large.

These girls change about five times a day. They dress for every meal and they put beach clothes on then some of them have riding habits (is that spelled right?).

So you've learned to ride a bike after all these years. How many times did you fall?

Are you insinuating that I'm returning with a family? I don't like that at all. Tell me you didn't mean it.

The dance was nice but I didn't care to dance much—it was too hot.

I'm very busy at the hotel and I don't get out much.

Keep the sunshine off your nose.

"Luke"

The Letters

    The African Methodist Episcopal (AME) Church started in Philadelphia in the late 1700s. In the 1800s, it spread to Pennsylvania towns like Wilkes-Barre that had small populations of African Americans.

    My mother often reminisced about the picnics when members of the area's AME churches would gather at Rocky Glen Park. When I asked my cousin Amanda Chattam (a descendant of Frank and Hattie Parks) if she recalled the picnics, she replied, "How well I remember the annual picnic. From all around people would come to Rocky Glen. We would go on the train about fifteen miles up the road around nine or ten in the morning and come back home about seven in the evening. Everyone would have big picnic baskets full of fried chicken, homemade cakes, and pies. We young people would love to see the other young people from different towns and cities. The older people who were too old for the rides would sit in the covered sheds and play checkers or other games and probably gossip about other people. By the time I got to be around twelve, the park closed. The churches were also splitting up so that was the end of the annual picnic."

    Cab Calloway was one of the most successful bandleaders of the 1930s and '40s and was famous for his flamboyant style. Beginning in 1931, his group was the house orchestra at Harlem's Cotton Club. The orchestra also toured Europe and appeared in several films.

Wilkes-Barre, Pa
July 15, 1937
Dear Luke,

    Hasn't this heat been terrific? The folks say it has made me just a bit dizzy. A new boy in town has given me the nickname of "Flighty." He thinks it is so appropriate.

    We have been having loads of fun bicycle-riding, car-riding and dancing. The kids from Scranton come down a couple of times a week. Chris was home and took Rudy and Sara and I riding. Rudy was one half hour late for work so we weren't on speaking terms when we got home. Chris made up a new song in honor of the occasion. It's called "Sore-head." Think you'd like to hear it?

Goodness, Luther, do you know that summer is flying swiftly by and I haven't begun to even think about a job. If I don't start looking soon I won't be able to go on any vacation because my Dad will think I don't need it. We don't get up until noon and then it's too hot to bother about anything. Mary said as soon as her Dad got their car simonized maybe we'd go see about some jobs. But we decided it's too hot to sit three in a seat, so that's off.

Everyone is talking about the picnic at Rocky Glen on the 29th. Cab Calloway is going to be there that night, but not for us. I guess we won't have any dance. The boogies will all be at the other dance looking in the windows (sad case). I hope the cops chase them down so we can have a little dance.

Mary

"Me on a bike"

My nose isn't shiny thank you.

Asbury Park
7-19-37
Dear Mary,

    I hope you are recovering from this intense heat—at least I hope you are no longer dizzy. If that strange boy can't nickname you better than that tell him not to even try.

    It's swell to hear you are having lots of frolic while I'm working from early morning until late at night but the folks are nice so I don't mind much. I still haven't been over to town events very often. I go to the boardwalk very often—it's only a block away.

    Tell Chris to run down some time in the week day and let me know. If you were down here last week I could have gotten you a job right next door to the hotel I'm working at. The lady asked me if I could get her a nice girl. I asked her how long she could wait until she came but she wanted her the next day. You couldn't have come down in a day!

    I hope you all will enjoy the picnic and I also hope it isn't as cold as last year because I won't be there to give you my coat and I don't want anyone else to lend you one.

    I thought that Sara was the artist in your family. She's almost draws as well as you do.

    Tell the family I said hello.

"Luke"

Wilkes–Barre, Pa.
July 22, 1937
Dear Luke,

After all my talk about the heat I have caught a terrible cold. I'm glad you're not here to see me now, my face is swollen from fever and all I do is take pills. Isn't that lovely when I was having so much fun? (Oh yeah!)

We can't go bicycling anymore because Sara hurt her knee and had to have four stitches put in. My Dad says if he has to spend any more money for a doctor we won't get to the picnic. And that would be tragic.

I hope, too, it won't be cold because I wouldn't want to borrow anyone else's coat but yours.

<u>Please</u> <u>Don't</u> <u>Work</u> <u>Too</u> <u>Hard</u> even if the people are nice. I couldn't have it if you came home thin from overwork.

My eyes are so swollen I can't see to write anymore so you will excuse the shortness of this missive.
"The Barber's Daughter"
Mary Amore

P.S. Sara is helping me out by writing this little note. MEB

(Written on a torn piece of paper)

Just a note
Hello Luke,

How are ya? When are you coming back so I can chase you home? It's hot here and I'm getting terribly thin. Mary is getting fat. Well so long. I haven't anything else to tell you. Be good. Don't let the girls gibe you. Excuse paper but I don't like to waste a whole sheet for you. How's that bud from Fla.? Is he cute?

Sara

Asbury Park, N.J
July 26, 1937
Dear Barber's Daughter,

How is your cold? I hope it is better. You can't take it.

Sorry to hear of Sara's accident—also, I hope you can make the picnic. It won't be long now—just a matter of hours. Tell me about the picnic when you answer this letter. Tell Sara if she can't write a whole letter don't write at all. She is a reckless bicyclist—that's what she is.

The Florida boy is cute and he has a "mussy," you know a little hair over his upper lip and under his nose.

The nights have been very pleasant down here. We had a full moon three nights last week. It was beautiful hanging over the ocean. The ocean was very rough last week-end and you could hear it roaring while you were in bed. It sounds awfully weird at night.

I can't sleep late because we have about seven or eight children staying here and they get up early and come to my room and wake me up. I have to raise the flag every morning so I told them the first one up puts the flag up so now they get up five-thirty and six o'clock just to put the flag up.

Well my dear, have a nice time at the picnic and be careful.
"Luke"

17 N. State St.
Wilkes-Barre, Pa.
Aug. 1, 1937
Dear Luke,

Did you wish me bad luck or what? I almost didn't get to that picnic. I honestly believe someone has the jinx on me. Can you imagine three days before the picnic and I had to go to bed with a bad attack of the grippe. The doctor wouldn't even let me eat.

But Thursday morning I got out of that bed and I ate and I went to the picnic and I'm none the worse for wear outside of being a little tired. I went back to bed on Friday until that evening I got up and went to the show. Saturday, I went back to bed and then went to a party that night. We didn't get to bed until nearly four o'clock. I ate my breakfast today at two o'clock. I look like I have two black eyes but they will be alright soon, I hope.

This whole month has been a continual celebration, parties and outings and movies. Almost as good as a vacation.

Rudy has a 1929 Packard but since we're not on speaking terms he won't take me for a ride. I hope he gets plenty of flat tires, the hateful old thing. Chris has gone away again so that ends his car. Dear, if my Dad would buy one then we could go to that dance in Stroudsburg. We know some kids there but they're so countrified that the dried mud from their shoes causes too much dust.

I forgot to tell you Cab Calloway didn't come for the policeman's outing at Rocky Glen. So we didn't see him after all.

Luther, you don't want to let those kids get you down. Early rising will be good for you for a change.

Have you heard "Sweet Heartaches"? It's swell.
Mary

Hotel Alameda
One Block from the Ocean
207 Seventh Avenue
Asbury Park, N.J.

8-5-37

Dear Mary:

How is it you always have something wrong with you at the wrong time. You can't be living right. I think you are living to fast—too much gaiety—slow down please because when I come back you'll be too tired and worn out to talk to me.

I'm using some of the hotel stationary for a change. Is it alright by you? How are all the kids and were there any deaths, newborn babies or marriages since I left?

You shouldn't do Rudy that way. Now you can't ride in his car. Tell your brother thanks for his card. If he keeps on eating hot dogs, when I come back he'll be barking.

It seems as though the picnic dance was a flop any more. Well I'm sacrificing all dances and picnics until after Labor Day.

Tell your Dad to come down—I need a haircut.

Keep sweet,

"Luke"

Dear Mary, Dear Luther

My mother, at five feet two inches was the shortest among her siblings. All her life, she was sensitive about her height.

Wilkes-Barre, Pa
Aug. 10, 1937
Dear Luke,

Can you tell by my elegant penmanship that I am a year older since Sunday? I am now nineteen—going on twenty. Believe it or not! Sara's John had the nerve to ask me when I was going to grow up. I felt like pulling his permanent wave.

Guess what, we almost went to Philadelphia via Reading but Sara made a wise-crack about Jimmy T. and our Papa changed his mind. Was I burned up, then Sara always did talk too much, darn her.

Sorry, there have been no births nor marriages and glad there have been no deaths. But you can't imagine who is engaged—Evelyn Payne to Verne McCloe! She has a great big diamond and we're all very proud of it. Louise and Alec are still engaged. You may be surprised to learn they changed the wedding date from June to sometime in February. Alec became a little impatient. I saw Edgar P[atience] last night, he looked awfully sad. I wonder if he is disillusioned. His wife isn't a bit cheerful looking either. You never saw such a dead pan expression.

The bell-hops have been having a civil war over at the hotel between Griff and Johnny Lyles and the old man Redington. He fires the whole gang every other day. Today, Buddy Grimes took him up on it and stayed home. They phoned for him to come back and he did at ten o'clock. Trying to look independent. Poor bell-hops.

There was a party in Scranton last night. We had loads of fun. A priest called us to see if we wouldn't "just act like we were civilized and enjoy ourselves." We did "enjoy ourselves" immensely.

Well that covers the waterfront.

Keep sweet yourself.

Mary

The Letters

Asbury Park, N.J
8-13-37
Dear Mary,

So glad to hear you are at last growing up to be a fine young lady. Are you still arguing with John? That shows that you have childish ways about you yet.

How does it feel to almost go away? I guess that is the nearest you've ever been to leaving Wilkes-Barre except going to Scranton once. I see Papa is still the boss.

People up there don't care who they become engaged to. I'm waiting for you to tell me that Mary and Wash have been married or sumptin.'

Is Doc Reid still in Wilkes-Barre?

So the bell boys are going on a sit down strike. Well, it's being done now-a- days so they will be right in line with the present headlines. God bless them for they no not what they do.

So you have a priest to call on you—more competition. Does he give you holy advice and do you heed it?

Well Mary, congratulations on your nineteenth birthday and no other girl in the world could be so charming in only nineteen years—honest and truly.

"Luke"

Aug. 20, 1937
Wilkes-Barre, Penna.
Dear Luke,

Please forgive me for being so slow in writing to you. But it has been so hot here that it is misery to even eat and sleep. We're beginning to look sort of droopy. I've taken to shorts and halter necks (greek to you) to keep a little cooler.

Didn't you know that Howard had gone to Buffalo in June?

As for Mary and Wash that is a long story. Del [Washington Downey's mother] found a letter Mary had written to Wash. She gave it to Georgie [Mary Buster's mother] and then the trouble began. Georgie wanted Griff [Mary's stepfather] to have the "nigger" arrested and poor Mary cried bucketfuls. When she found out that Wash hadn't anything to say in her defense she wished she had the courage to shoot him in the leg. I almost died laughing at her.

But it is all blown over and Mary still thinks Wash has everything. He is in Pittsburgh now. Louise says he doesn't like it out there but Del wants him to stay away for now.

Can you imagine my mother said I could go to Scranton for my vacation? I told her I'd better go to Kingston and then she could yell when she wanted me.

Almost forgot to tell you that Catherine Carter and Jimmy Wynder were married today. They are celebrating at Breezes. I think they were certainly slow enough about it, don't you?

Art Sands has gone away, too. So has my brother, but just until Monday. He rec'd his vacation this week.

"Are you newsy Mary bored stiff?"

The Letters

The late night fire my father writes about was covered extensively in northern newspapers including 'The New York Times'. The heat from the fire was so intense it forced onlookers to stand a block away. The glow from the flames could be seen from miles away. Fortunately, no one was seriously injured but many hotel guests were left with nothing to wear but their night clothes.

Hotel Alameda
One Block from the Ocean
207 Seventh Avenue
Asbury Park, N.J.

Aug. 27 - 37

Dear Mary,

I don't see why you have been in misery from the heat when we manage to keep so cool and collected. As far as shorts and halters, are concerned, that is all I see worn from the time I get up until I go to bed. It even has become old-fashioned already to me.

You don't mean to tell me that there is still a W-B Pa with Doc, Wash, Art and your brother out of it? It's a wonder they didn't throw the key to the city away. As for Mary and Wash all good things must have an ending. It's a wonder Georgia didn't have the Supreme Court try Wash and have him executed.

Scranton is far enough for a little girl to go away from her mother and father so you just go like a nice girl and watch when you cross the streets.

I seem to be in great demand for this winter. The people I'm working for now want to take me to Fla. Some people that live here want me to come to Conn., and I got two offers to work in New York City but I haven't made up my mind yet.

We had lots of excitement down here last Saturday night. Two hotels burned down right near the one I'm working in now. Some of our guests became excited and I had to carry their belongings out on the sidewalk. They were hollering, "I'm next Luke" and some of them were arguing about me. Did I feel important but about an hour later the fire was under control and I had to carry all the things back in the hotel—not so happy about that and was I mortified.

We had a rainy spell since Saturday. All they do now is play games in the hotel. So when I get back I have lots of new games we can play when the gang congregates.

Well Mary, I'll see you in my dreams,
"Luke"

The Letters

Sept. 2, 1937
Wilkes-Barre, Pa
Dear Luke,

It was "simply grande" reading about your popularity. I read about the fire in the paper. Sorry your name wasn't mentioned for your heroic work with the luggage. It might have been some compensation to see your name in print after all that struggle.

So they are still trying to get you to go to Fla. The old meanies. Please make up your mind what you're going to do, the suspense is terrible.

It is still so hot here you can scarcely breathe. I hope I lose some weight, the folks say I'm getting sort of plump and that will never do. I'll be looking like Sara and Mary B. if I don't watch out.

Saturday we're going to Harding to a wiener roast. Florence Glover is giving it and she has invited both gangs from Scranton and W – B. It looks like loads of fun. On Monday, there is a dance in Scranton which we don't want to miss. I'm being a very good girl. That ought to help.

Art has come home for a week and my brother is home so we didn't have to throw the key to the city away after all. But don't worry we girls aren't perishing from loneliness. We still can play "Tiddley Winks" and "Bingo" and we get marvelous practice dancing with each other. When you come home we can give you the fine points of all three.

The taffy you sent is delicious. We chew taffy and imagine we're at the beach. Isn't the imagination a wonderful thing?

Thanks loads and loads.
Mary

[Post-marked September 9, 1937]
409 Edgecombe Ave.
New York City
New York

Dear Mary,

You cannot tell from where you'll hear from me. It's apt to be India, Norway or Galappi where ever that is.*

I had to escape from Asbury because the people I worked for seemed as though they wanted to adopt me. Take note that I always live on an avenue when I live in a city.

I arrived in N.Y. Thursday evening and came to Emily's apartment and Rosabelle Downey was there. Emily had two pork chops in the pan when I came in so I told her she had to be better than that. I gained eight pounds in Asbury but I guess I'll lose all that in N.Y.

I'm going to paint the town red if I don't run out of paint. Those buildings are very high.

I'll be here for about two weeks then I'm coming home. I may work in New York this winter. I'll know better later on.

My address is

Mr. Luther Snyder

c/o Busch Apt 1F

409 Edgecombe Ave.

New York, NY

And I still think you're the grandest person I've ever met.

"Luke"

*My father was referring to Gallipoli. The Battle of Gallipoli took place in Turkey during World War I. British and French forces tried to capture Istanbul, at the time the capital of the Ottoman Empire. The attempt failed, with many deaths on both sides.

The Letters

Much later in her life, after raising her children, taking care of my father during his long illness, and retiring from work, my mother began painting. I never knew until reading this letter that she was fulfilling a long-postponed dream to be an artist.

Sept. 14, 1937
Wilkes-Barre
Dear Luke,

I was in Scranton when your letter arrived (my vacation). But it was swell to come home and read that you're thinking of coming home. Goodness it seems like you've been gone a year instead of several months. We probably won't know each other and have to be introduced but I hope not.

Well school has started and I'm still unemployed. I've had several offers but they're not what I want so I just don't accept. But I hope I get one soon or my Dad says back to school for me (calamity).

Luke, please don't paint N.Y. too red because you know I have hopes to show my artistic ability and I don't want that chance spoiled. So please remember that.

Don't forget that when you live in this city you live on a street. You may get in the wrong residence when you come home if you forget.

Waiting patiently
Mary

In 1937, Ella Fitzgerald was still early in her career. She had won an amateur contest at the Apollo Theater in Harlem in 1934, which led to an engagement with Chick Webb's band and regular performances at the Savoy Ballroom.

Don Redman played saxophone and was a Big Band leader. He also wrote for many of the jazz greats of the 1930s and '40s and later was Pearl Bailey's musical director.

The Lindy Hoppers were a popular swing dance troupe that performed at the Savoy Ballroom and other New York venues. They performed one of their sensational dance routines in the Marx Brother's zany 1937 film, "A Day at the Races." The web page 'SavoyStyle.com' attributes the Lindy Hoppers with influencing dance styles around the world.

New York City
Sept. 20, 1937
Dear Mary,

So you spent your vacation in beautiful sunny Scranton—how swell that must have been.

It's sort of swell in the city because a lot of Wilkes-Barrians are down here—every time I go out I meet one and it took me a week to call on them. Charlie is a roundabout.

It's a thrill riding down to Times Square on a double decker bus. I go down in the morning and come back in the late afternoon. I go to the show then to the art museum and to the aquarium then to Radio City. There are so many places of interest down here. Charlie and a friend of mine with his wife and Charlie's girl and a girlfriend went to a chop suey joint the other night and had oodles of fun.

The hotel where Charlie works may hire me sometime in the near future but I'm not sure of that yet.

All New York is swing crazy. I saw and heard Ella Fitzgerald—she is very clever. I went to the Apollo and saw Wesley Bunch in Don Redman's Big Apple Revue last week. Then to the famous Savoy Ballroom and the Harvest Moon Lindy Hoppers were there. You should see the cutting up they do.

As for myself I'm sort of a sentimentalist you know. Listen to "So Rare"—it's my favorite and so are you.

"Luke"

In this letter, following a visit home to Wilkes-Barre, Luther reminisces about when he met my mother as part of a wedding procession at Wilkes-Barre's Bethel AME Church.

New York City
Sept. 29 – 37
Dear Mary,

It was swell to return to the city—but I really did regret leaving you again. I hope that something can be done about that. Note that I am using green ink because green means go.

Tuesday night I went to a wedding with some friends of mine. I think it's the first wedding I have even attended except the wedding at which I was honored to have you as a partner in the procession one night at the church. I think that started my acquaintance with you—how thrilling. I haven regretted that night one bit so help me. So much for the weddings.

I have been a few places since I came back but I won't tell you since it makes you feel so badly, really I can't blame you and truly regret you can't have the same privilege.

My address now is:
L.W. Snyder
c/o Winfield Apt. 1b
225 W. 146 Street
New York City

Please tell Mary B. to tell Griff as soon as possible to send my formal clothes to me and you give them the address of Mrs. Busch where I stayed last time please.

Stay charming
"Luke"

The Letters

P.S. I forgot something very important—Sonny. He's the rascal of the neighborhood but a darn good fellow. He dances and sings and is a natural born humorous. Jimmy Lunceford lives in this apartment house also and he thinks that Sonny is a wonder. When he comes home next time he'll take you out.

In my Saturday night galavant I met Harriet Oliver and she asked me about you. I told her as much as I could without seeing you in so long. I have an infected eye and it's being treated by a doctor. I wear dark glasses sometime but not for the sun and it was bandaged up also. It's getting better now.

I think I'll be home Friday. If I don't I'll let you know. I think I'll have to return to NY Monday so I'll see you soon.
"Luke"

Oct. 4, 1937

Dear Luke,

It was swell of you to use green ink signifying go. It is encouraging. Poor me—I have been "panned" to death about going to N.Y. John Foster told me the mosquitoes on Times Square would eat me up. When I enquired where they would come from, my dear mother said from the meadows nearby. Do I look that green to you?

Please forget all the mean things I said about Flossie Roach's Sam. He is positively the grandest person. He has invited Sara, Flossie and me to spend Christmas at his house in Allenville. It's about 108 miles from N.Y. The dear thing thinks it will be some compensation for not going to N.Y. But in case we don't like Allenville he will gladly show us N.Y. Bless his heart.

My mother is so tired of me wanting to go away she is trying her best to get me a job so I'll have something else to think about. She has one in view for me now. Here's hoping.

Luke, I haven't seen Mary Buster in ages so you'd better write to Griff about your formal clothes. Just in case.

We're taking cooking lessons now and swimming lessons. So when I go to the beach in 1965 I'll know how to swim.

"Travelorn"

Mary

The Letters

This is the first mention of the Brown family: siblings Harry, Lois, and Evelyn (Evie). Harry Brown eventually married my mother's youngest sister, Lillian, affectionately referred to in these letters as Sister. My father took French in high school and includes a word or phrase now and then.

[Post-marked October 8, 1937]
225 W. 146 St.
N.Y.C.
Dear Mary,

It was grand to hear from you but much better to see you. Quit holding out on me will ya.

Lois Brown, Harry and Evie his sister were down Saturday (last). Harry slept all day—he couldn't take it. Lois came over to my residence and my friend and his wife with Lois went out until 4 a.m. Sunday morning. I'll stay in the rest of the week, I said, but went to a dance Monday night.

Listen Mary, don't let those country folks ride you so much because I think you are a "hip chick", by the way that is some of the slang that is used down hear. That means the girl is very wise and smart. You had better get a job and then you can come whenever you get ready. Just let me know when. Stop pestering your mother—she is doing the best she can I'm sure.

I could go to a swell dance Sat. night (Oct 9) but I didn't receive my clothes so I don't think I'll go. I'll sit home and meditate about you.

I got a letter from Art Thursday but I don't know how he got my address. He may come down here Sunday. I suppose that means [an] all night affair. When the hometown folks get together down here we make it a gala night.

Well until next time I guess it's

Au revoir

"Luke"

Oct. 15, 1937

Dear Luke,

I think I must be slightly in a fog. I spend my days doing simply daffy things. I wrote to you a few days ago and put the wrong address on the envelope. This morning the letter returned. I think it must have been all over the city of N.Y. Better luck next time.

Arthur Sands was home this week. By the way—he wrote me some time ago asking for your address. I hope you didn't mind my sending it to him. He says he goes to your city about every week.

Did you know that Wash was in Rochester now? Everybody will be in N.Y. somewhere by Christmas. Make it seem like good old PA.

Can you imagine it snowing here already? Didn't have time to air my red flannels this year. Terrible, I say.

Griff and his wife are at home now. They are trying to get a new job for the next few weeks. Keeps Mary busy trying to remember where they are half the time, they change so often.

Harry Brown was up to tell me all about his trip. He even bragged about the nice rest he had while there. He says he doesn't like N.Y. But he's already planning another visit. Trying to make me jealous. The Old Greeny.

Thank you for saying I'm so wise and smart, Luke, it helps me a lot.
Mary

The Letters

The avenue my father mentions is the section of Seventh Avenue north of Central Park, a main street in Harlem. Today, it is officially called Adam Clayton Powell Jr. Boulevard after the Baptist minister and Congressman who represented Harlem from 1945 to 1971.

Oct 22, 1937
New York City
Dear Mary:

What sort of disease do you suffer, the loss of memory? I hope you don't forget your name.

It was quite alright to give Art my address but I couldn't imagine how he got it. I haven't seen hide nor hair of him as yet.

I suppose Wash's next step will be here. I hope, I hope, I hope! I won't be satisfied seeing everyone here unless you are included.

Sometimes I think the Wrights are haunting me. I see them every time I go down the avenue. They look like a bunch of farmers.

We haven't witnessed snow here yet but it has been cool but very clear. I wrote to Griff and if he asks you the address to send the parcel, give him 409 Edgecombe Ave, apt 1F c/o Busch. Thank you. No one is home here during the day therefore no one could receive the parcel but at my cousin's there is someone home day and night.

Tell the family I said hello, including Sara.

By the way is there any castle you want me to build Baby?
"Luke"

Oct. 27, 1937

Dear Luke,

Well here I am in dear ol' Scranton, again, just having a "mellow" time. It's the most sleepy little town on the map besides W.B., believe me. They are having a Halloween dance here Monday. I hope it wakes them up.

Do you know Maxine Cunningham? Well, she has a baby girl. Norman Jones is up here sick in the hospital. He has tuberculosis and pneumonia. They don't expect him to get well. By the way Griff is working up here in the Hotel Casey. I guess they are going to move up here, although your friend Mary doesn't want to.

Luke, I am surprised at you making fun of your home town friends. Can they help it if they look like farmers? Don't forget that after all they are from Lincoln St. and they aren't used to civilized ways. Just give them time, they'll learn. I just dare anyone to call me "farmer" or "greeny" when I come to N.Y. It'll be the sorriest thing they ever said and I mean it. So you just prepare everyone when you hear that I'm coming—save me the trouble.

Flossie, Sara and I have made all kinds of plans but heaven knows when we'll get to N.Y. Everybody here is talking about it. They think we're much too young to come to such a big city. I just say "Phooey" and let it go at that. You know my stubbornness personified. My mother should have called me Hard!

And please don't build me any castles—just a "Penthouse on Third Ave." I love them just a few stories high.

Mary

The Letters

Nov. 2, 1937

Dear Mary,

I am writing this letter before breakfast so if the writing appears to be a little weak you'll know why. I always did like to exercise before breakfast—you can eat so much more.

I sincerely hope you had a swell time at the dance last night. I bet the cats were jumpin', the roof rockin' and the neighbors knockin'.

I already had received the news of the newborn babies, Maxine's, and Edgar's wife. There is some action up there at that—excuse it please.

It sounds pretty bad for Norman—he has my sympathy. It is a task to keep up with Griff Reynolds. He seems to like variety very much—Mary has to string along I suppose.

Imagine meeting Beville on the avenue one night, then Greenie the tailor the next night, then lo and behold who should ring the doorbell last Friday night—and me answering it standing before me grinning—Art Sands. I had my pajamas and robe on, just about ready to retire because it was 11:00 p.m. He had about six boys with him but they stayed in the car. He was going to the Savoy Ballroom and his friends didn't have ties so I supplied them with accessories.

Is there anyone in W-B besides you and Sara all week long? The Wrights caught me again. Next time I meet them I'll scream. My clean cut ex-neighbors.

I already told everybody you were a city chick in a hick town so your name is already made—all you've got to do is live up to it.

Listen, don't tell anyone else you want a penthouse on Third Avenue because that is where the slums are. You want a penthouse on Park Avenue or at least Edgecombe Ave. I wish you could see Third Avenue—it's the bowery.

Well that is all the news this time but more next time—until then a cheerio

"Luke"

Although my mother used this letter to flaunt her popularity, this letter also reflects both the aspirations and achievement of African American men and the burdens carried by African American men in racist areas of America.

According to its website, Lincoln University was the first educational institute in the U.S. founded for education of Black males. Its graduates include the poet Langston Hughes, Supreme Court Justice Thurgood Marshall, and Kwame Nkrumah, the first president of Ghana.

The town of Nanticoke is about ten miles south of Wilkes-Barre.

Wilkes-Barre, Pa
11/8/37
Dear Luke,

My traveling career has begun. I spent ten whole days in Scranton plus one night in Kingston. Don't you envy me. Sara does. She hasn't been away anywhere since last summer—poor child. Wait until she's nineteen going on twenty.

By the way Andy MacDonald was here from Philadelphia. He brought two college fellows from Lincoln with him. I was in Scranton at the time but Sara said she had a "salubrious" time. Andy wants her to come to Philadelphia for a football game and dance. I guess she will be going. She has the permission already (Don't faint—it's true.)

Beville told me that he saw you in N.Y. He goes there about twice a month. Also, Art Sands wrote me of his visit to the "big town." He wants Louise and Alec to bring me to Newburg some time this winter. The way he talks it must be kind of mellow. I hope—I hope—I hope.

Can you imagine there were about fifteen boys at our house yesterday (Sunday). And only the three Brooks sisters to entertain—but we did have loads of fun. I feel all in today. It is a strain—this popularity of ours (ego).

The Letters

Have you heard the latest? Flossie Roach and Niles are so close you'd think they were Siamese twins—really you would. Also all the colored boys were politely asked not to come to Nanticoke any more. They were very indignant but it has blown over and forgotten—practically.

Are you hinting that everyone has gone away and left us? Or what?
Mary

Curiously, my father didn't comment on the Nanticoke situation.

225 W. 146 St.
N.Y.C.
Nov. 15, 37
Dear Mary,

Doesn't traveling just bore you? I imagine it does. Tell Sara I'm having a great big laugh about her going to Philadelphia but still hope she does go. I'm sure she needs the change of atmosphere and I don't mean the weather.

Edgar Patience has been down here since last Thursday so he and I have been mixing business with pleasure. We had a sort of reunion down here yesterday (Sunday). Edgar Greenie and his new bride and myself went to the museum of natural art—then for a ride.* We had dinner at the house I stay at, after attending a very good colored show. Rosabelle came to the house, then it turned into a party. Later we saw Harriet Oliver and Clinton, also Mrs. Foster.

The day had all the earmarks of a day in Wilkes-Barre except a few little [things] that we'll look over.

If you make your trip to Newburg will you be so kind as to stop by here so I can say hello to you? As far as it being mellow here, the city speaks for itself.

Perhaps the reason for your popularity is because they have no other pickings to molest. But I reckon you all are very popular no less, don't lose it.

"Luke"

My father was probably referring to the Museum of Natural History.

Pianist and band leader Claude Hopkins was well-known to 1930s jazz and swing fans. He studied music and medicine at Howard University. During his career, he worked as music director for famed entertainer Josephine Baker.

Wilberforce University, an African Methodist Episcopal Church University located in Ohio, is the nation's oldest private, historically Black university. It was named to honor William Wilberforce, the 18th century British abolitionist.

11/22/37

Dear Luke,

Well since winter is really here I guess my traveling career is ending. Too cold for me to venture out much now. But I do believe that you see more of the W – B folks than I do even if it is cold and everyone is supposed to be staying home.

I have been pretty busy lately doing nothing as usual. I did work two days last week substituting for another girl.* I burned myself and cut my finger so bad it was bandaged for nearly a week. But Archer said that everything was "elegante." The first day I was there he called me "Kid" and "Toots." But I soon put him in his place and he finally learned my name was Mary.

There was a group of kids here from Wilberforce University last week. They certainly did sing beautifully. After the concert the singers and our crowd all went over to Foster's and had a mellow time. There were ten boys and two girls.

There are five dances here and in Scranton this week. None to brag about except on Friday Claude Hopkins will be in Scranton. Since Sara heard about it she decided not to go to Philadelphia. If you ask me she didn't intend to go anyway. She was only trying to make me jealous. But I wasn't in the least bit interested—much.

Don't eat too much for Thanksgiving.
Mary

*My mother's first job was as a coat check attendant at a country club. Her burn was not related to her job.

The Letters

Hotel Wellington
Seventh Avenue
Fifty-Fifth and Fifty-Sixth Streets
New York

N.Y.C
Nov. 29, 1937
Dear Mary,

It is swell to know that I can find you home if I should call. I didn't know where you were half the time. I just trusted to luck to find you at home.

Please excuse my writing I'm a little shaky this afternoon for no good reason at all.

After I received your last letter and read it I went out and <u>dad blame it</u>, I run into a Wright. I'm about to surrender to them.

Sorry to hear of your injury I hope it heals soon. So the zegg was getting wise with you. Well I should come up there and punch him in his big mouth. How big is he?

I guess I've been officially named "Freckles" down here. A lot of girls and fellows seem to know me better by that name than my right name.

How was the dance Friday night? Did Claude Hopkins rock and did the cats jump?

I hope that you and the family had a very lovely Thanksgiving. I did.

"Luke"

Dec. 6, 1937
Dear Luke,

This writing is so wobbly you may not be able to read it. But I'm balancing a box of writing paper on my knee and that accounts for it and not a chill.

I saw Edgar P. and he told me of the wonderful time he had while visiting you. Nellie Mabine is also bubbling over with news of N.Y. She is going to be here until Christmas. She's so small I thought she'd be stepped on in all the rush, but she seems to do O.K.

By the way we saw Harriet Oliver's picture in the colored journal. She was pictured as a ballet dancer and she certainly seemed to have poise. If you see her give her my congrats.

We were up to Downey's the other day when Rose and Minnie called their mother. Mrs. Downey was worried because someone had told her Charlie was hurt. It was a big relief when the girls called.

We were away for Thanksgiving, but by the names of the people who were here while we were gone I wish that we had stayed home. Ben Johnson was here with a friend from N.Y. the Saturday following and I wasn't home—worse luck. Sarah said he oozed good manners—and awful sharp. She was all aflutter—but you know Sarah.*

Well, Sister has something for me and I just must see what it is, so "Addios, Aloha"

Marie

Regards to the Wrights

My aunt spelled her name Sara, as my mother did in most of the letters. For some reason, she added an 'h' in this letter, a mistake my father often made.

The Letters

My mother's family lived across the street from a police station. Not having a phone of their own, they often used the police station telephone to make calls.

Dec. 11, 1937
Dear Mary,

How are you and all your copper neighbors? I suppose they have ceased to pose out in front of their beloved hoosegow*. Tell them I send my love. The Hellman's are down here but we can't seem to contact. They go where I ain't and I go where they have just left, but I [can't] catch them yet. They don't know my address.

Did you go to the dance in Scranton to hear Claude Hopkins? I heard they romped and stomped until break of day.

You would be away when someone interesting calls to your house.

Does Sara beat her drum very much or is Clarence using it. Did you eat your lolly-pops? I should demand one myself. Tell all the folks I said hello.

Sonny is still dancing—he can do the rhumba now. I must conclude but hope I hear from you soon.
"Luke"

*According to the Random House "Maven's Word of the Day", October 28, 1997, hoosegow is an anglicized version of the Spanish word for jail, juzgado.

In 1937, Count Basie was just beginning the climb to his eventual stature as a prominent big band leader with the release of "One O'Clock Jump" on the Decca label.

Dec. 17, 1937
Dear Luke,

I was certainly surprised when I read your letter asking about the dear police neighbors. I am very glad to be able to write that they are fine and hope you are the same. Amen. They were ever so pleased to think that you remembered them. They asked me to tell you that the police station has been painted inside and out and all new doors are being put on the garage side facing us. More police news next time. (They're busy.)

The lolly-pops have not been eaten and I'll be sure to save you a nice red one if and when I do eat them. Sara's drum is put away for posterity—lucky kids; so Clarence is out of luck for rehearsing, thank heavens.

Sorry to say I did not attend the Claude Hopkins affair—the rest of the family did, although, and they said it was O.K. Count Basie is supposed to be here for Christmas and I hope I'll be able to attend this one. After four weeks I finally got rid of a terrible cold. For a while I looked like a prize fighter—

Tell Sonny to be sure to save a dance for me when I visit him. I hope he won't be too old. I'm learning to truck now slowly but surely—tell Sonny. The rhumba is next for his sake.
Mary

The Letters

Russ Morgan was a popular 1930's musician and bandleader, lesser known today than some of the other artists mentioned in these letters.

Dec 22, 1937
N.Y.C.
Dear Mary:

Nice hearing from you. I suppose you and the family are all aflutter about the approaching holidays. Have you got a Christmas tree this year? Don't forget to hang your stocking up.

Since the police station has made those improvements all they need to make it complete is a new police force, you tell them.

Chris was home waiting for me one evening when I arrived. He still is Chris. We went out and we stopped at a place to talk and he entertained and he thought he saw a girl resembling Sara. He almost jumped out of his skin.

I went to hear Russ Morgan the other day. He was grand—in fact the whole show was superb.

Well here is hoping and wishing you all a sincerely joyful Christmas.
"Luke"

Dec. 28, 1937

Dear Luke,

I don't know whether it was your good wishes or not but we had a very lovely Christmas. Your candy was appreciated to the utmost and a thousand thanks for your remembrance.

You can imagine our surprise when Ben Johnson, Wash, Andy, Chalky, Rose and Minnie plus a dozen or more of visitors were here for the holiday. They were calling at our house every few minutes. We were thinking of hiring a doorman for the time being. Most of the people were from N.Y. and I learned plenty about the "Big Town" in the last few days.

I have to go to work tonight at 7:30 so I'll have to make this a short one. I'm a very busy person, worked all last week including Christmas day and didn't even get my Christmas shopping done, alas.

Hoping you enjoyed your Christmas as much.

I'll sign off.

Mary

1938

The Great Depression dragged on in 1938. The American economy, which had been slowly recovering from its low point in 1933, took a sharp downturn in mid-1937. Unemployment jumped from around 14 percent in 1937 to 19 percent in 1938. This impacted my father, who was laid off near the end of the year.

Luther continued to sublet a room in an apartment for housing. During the Depression, many families rented rooms to single men. It provided much needed low-cost housing for the men and generated extra cash for the landlord.

Hotel Wellington
Seventh Avenue
Fifty-Fifth and Fifty Sixth Streets
New York

Jan. 4, 1937*
Dear Mary,

    Hearing of your lovely Christmas only makes me feel that I should enjoy mine more. It's nice you liked the candy. You know my motto, sweets to the sweet. Thank your Mother, Father, Sisters and Brother for their lovely Holiday Greetings.

    I'm sorry I couldn't join the others in returning home for Christmas but the time allotted me wasn't enough. Perhaps I can come home for my birthday, it is a holiday also. I don't know why the President chose the same day as mine to have a birthday but I couldn't refuse after he asked me. Just think you'll be another year older this year!

    Start asking your parents if you can attend a formal down here in April. They'll be some before that but I'm afraid you will not get up enough courage to ask to come before then. I guarantee it will be a Sender Mr. Bender if you can come. Well more next time.

"Luke"

*My father mistakenly wrote the wrong year.

Jan, 10, 1938
Dear Luther,

It was nice hearing from you again. I want to thank you for asking me to your formal and Sara. I am sure it will be all that you say. You can be certain I shall do my very hardest coaxing between now and April.

Howard Reid surprised everyone and came home on New Year's Day. He called at our house but I was not at home and therefore I didn't see him. But they say he looked well for all of his hard work. By the way how is Art Sands? I haven't seen nor heard of him since before Thanksgiving. Everyone around here is asking about him.

Mrs. Haley introduced us to your cousin Clarence when he was here. He certainly is very nice looking—in case you might like to know. I can hear Davey crying over at Mrs. Haley's—he and Emily are getting ready to leave, I guess. He's so bashful he won't talk to me. Were you ever so bashful, I wonder?

Luther, it would be very, very grand if you will come home for your birthday, and in case you might like to know in eight months I will be <u>20!</u> Doesn't time fly?

Mary

The Letters

Benny Goodman was a clarinetist and jazz musician known as the 'King of Swing.' As reported on 'Benny Goodman.com', his hugely successful quartet was the first jazz ensemble to perform in New York's Carnegie Hall. The quartet included African American vibraphonist Lionel Hampton.

Tommy Dorsey, a trombonist, was also a popular 1930's jazz musician. His orchestra was renowned for its ability to play both swing music and smooth ballads.

Seventh Avenue
Fifty-Fifth and Fifty-Sixth Streets
New York

1-17–38

Dear Mary,

    I received your missive with loads of glee. I really hope you can attend the formal in April. I told Mrs. Winfield you might come. She and her husband are very swell people, you'll like them and they are young. We have loads of fun at the house and lots of nice company. I hope you try very hard to come.

    It would have been quite a treat to see "Doc" Reid again. Does he talk as much as ever? Andy wrote to Charlie and said that he saw you. I haven't seen hide nor hare of Art perhaps he was exiled. My cousins and I were talking about home for two or three hours but we only repeated our statements over and over again.* No news is good news.

    I also talked to cousin Clarence, Charlie, Chris, and I talk of coming home but that seems to be all the closer we get. So [one] day out of a clear blue sky I'll blow into town, when I do not know.

    This hotel I work at is exactly like the Redington except larger, more exclusive. There are forty-eight bellboys. They wear snappy maroon uniforms with white gloves. There are seven elevators. We have an orchestra every night and a very beautifully decorated lobby. It's strange to have a hotel almost like the Redington down here and me get a job and feel right at home.

Well I suppose you don't care about the hotel but I just thought you could tell Clarence to come down and get a job.

I wish you were down here next week to see Benny Goodman, he really kills you.

Tommy Dorsey was a sender also.

Well get older and wiser.

Luke

My father was referring to Emily and her husband.

The Letters

Jan 24, 1938

Dear Luther,

Your very nice letter was rec'd with appreciation. I told my brother about your elegant hotel and those snappy maroon uniforms. He was green with envy. He has been having much trouble lately. He is getting too fat for his uniform. He has been the night man at the hotel since Oct. and Mr. Davies wears his trousers during the day. They have been taking turns having them mended. So you can easily see why he envies you.

He says look for him any time because he's disgusted….so am I. He sleeps all day and we can't even play the radio until evening….you can imagine what life must be like.

Sara works for Jewish people and her whole conversation is Zish and Isador (he's the son). She is hardly ever home anymore as she works at the Capital Theater at night…so I have to entertain myself.

The social activities of our fair town have increased somewhat and it keeps me busy keeping pace and socializing for the whole family. By the way your friends Olin and Tommie took me riding yesterday, Louise, and Blanche also. What did Tommy do but blunder something about the hateful party they gave. You should have seen the blank countenances—talk about golden silence—this was solid. Only silly Louise broke it by tittering.

Outside of that we had loads of fun. They wanted me to take in a movie but as I already had a date I had to decline the invite.

Well toodle loo until the next time.

Mary

My father's poignant expression of feeling "blue" is written the day after his twenty-seventh birthday.

Hotel Wellington
Seventh Avenue
Fifty-Fifth and Fifty-Sixth Streets
New York

Jan 31, 1938
NYC
Dear Mary,

It is about 1:30 pm of one of those melancholy days when you wish you were every where but the place you are. Ok, yes there are times when I feel as though I want to leave N.Y. also. I guess I'm just inclined to be a wanderer, but when I do feel that one it isn't for long because there is always something in this metropolis to distract my feelings.

I had a nice birthday—unexpected pleasure. I can't understand I haven't seen any of the Wrights for about three days. Surely they must be hibrinating or else they would let me see them.

Chris was to the house yesterday afternoon. He asked about Sarah. He would like her to answer his letter if she could spare the time. He'll never change. Sara is wearing him down. Since Sarah turned Yiddish I suppose she goes to the Synagogue on Saturday's or does she take advantage of all the social affairs? It helps the time to pass more quickly.

As you know time changes things. I'm sure you are hoping for some sort of change. Well have a lot of patience and strong hope, it may aid in your desire to leave your fair city.

By the way I'm not the voice of experience but an observer.
"Luke"

Feb. 7, 1938

Dear Luther,

You can be certain I appreciated the trouble you took to write those encouraging observations. I was sorry to read that you were feeling so low mentally, but I trust that all has passed and you are again your cheerful self.

I don't know what you would have done in this town this winter. We have had so little socially, I mean real fun, that I forget what a "good time" really means. We've had one dance here this winter. That was on Friday nite. It was over at 11:30 as it was the annual basketball dance at the Y.W.C.A. Incidentally we won 30-14 just in case you might like to know. So much for that.

Guess what? We are really going to Philadelphia this time—to a fraternity dance at Lincoln. Andy has so graciously invited both of us—bless his heart. He and Sara have been making plans all winter. Since Sara knows a few of the boys there she has me chock full of curiosity. Maybe that will be a beginning, I hope.

By the way Sara says to tell Chris she would write, but she can't just address the letter N.Y.C. because the post office authorities might not know Chris so well, so it would help if he would send an address.

My sincerest congratulations on your past birthday even though they are a little late.

Mary

The Millrose Games are an annual indoor track and field meet. The Games are held on the first Friday in February in New York City. At the 1938 Millrose Games, Ben Johnson broke the record for the 60-yard dash, finishing in 6.1 seconds. A short time later, he beat his own record, running the race in 6.0 seconds.

Hotel Wellington
Seventh Avenue
Fifty-Fifth and Fifty-Sixth Streets
New York

Feb. 15, 1938

Dear Mary,

    Well it won't be long now before you'll be planning to go to the Tonka Jacks annual dance and then the usual run of graduation parties will start. Then you all will be glad you are citizens of dear old W-B. I wonder if the Advocates will have their annual function. I would love to know. I'm very pleased to know that you excel in sports, especially basketball. Keep it up.

    I really hope I did not make an error in reading that you were going to Phila. Providing I didn't, I hope you will succeed and have a grand time. Please remember the environment will be entirely strange but don't feel out of place because you and your sister are swell company at anybody's fraternity dance. Please try to go and make the best of it. One dance for me please.

    I'm sure you've read about Ben Johnson in the newspaper. He's the tops.

    Please tell Sara I haven't seen Chris since I received your letter but I will tell him to send his address. Thanks loads for your hearty birthday congratulations.

    More next time.

"Luke"

The Letters

Feb. 22, 1938

Dear Luther,

Did you ever live thru a day when everything went absolutely wrong? Well this happens to be my bad luck day. First I simply couldn't wake myself up and stayed in bed too long for my mother's peace of mind. I burned my finger making toast, squirted orange juice in my eye, tore my best stockings and a hundred million other things. Poor me, it's wearing me down.

But I was compensated when my pal Mary B. dropped by for lunch and cheered me up. We hadn't had a real visit in three or four weeks. She lives in Lee Park since her mother and "Pote" work in Scranton.

We've been having a little excitement lately. A troupe of show people are boarding at Haley's—about seventeen of them I think. They practice everything from female impersonating to tap dancing. Some noise I must say, especially when they come in early in the morning.

By the way I must inform you that there are no more "Advocates" nor "Tonka Jacks." The clubs have entirely disbanded. But there is a new club in town, or rather at the S.S.Y. called the Phalanx. You've probably heard of it. Most Y.M.s have such a club, so I hear. I don't know whether they have planned an affair or not—they take after the S.S.S in a way (small way).

More next time.

Mary

Hotel Van Rensselaer
Eleventh Avenue near Fifth Avenue
New York

[Undated]

Dear Mary,

It was swell hearing from you but—please excuse the long delay in answering you but I have been busy lately. They delegated me to another hotel for a short time and the location from where I live is rather far.

I have been attending some nice formals lately also—wish you were here to enjoy them. We just pitch a ball. There are still some to come so you have an opportunity to attend one. I was the guest of Olin's brother Monday night.

So they are still giving Mary the run around. They can't do that to her. Bear in mind that if any club is organized it will never compare with the S.S.S. club because you all were different in every respect if you know what I mean.

Well there has been an increase in the family here at the house. Blessed events—an event sent here. It had to be a female too when all the time they wished for a little son. Well that's an uncontrollable action.

Take care of yourself and don't play the radio so loud—let Clarence snore.

"Luke"

The Letters

My mother finally leaves Wilkes-Barre to go to Philadelphia. It's such an exciting adventure, she sends home postcards!

March 14, 1938
Dear Luther,

It was a shock receiving your last missive. I thought maybe you had another attack of wanderlust and had gone to Gallipoli. It was good to know that you are still in N.Y.

Please don't think that I have deliberately delayed answering but I have been very busy. My popularity is beginning to wear me down, but one must keep up socially, so what can one expect.

We had the grandest time in Philadelphia. Sightseeing, dancing, nightclubbing, eating and what have you? Also were to Maryland. And N.J. We went to Md. after 3:30 in the morning so I don't recall much of what it looks like, except that we were there.

We had an awful time mailing our postal cards, in fact we mailed on our way home so you see we were pretty busy. Just had to let everyone know we were out of W-B no matter what.

Luther, you can imagine how pleased we were to see your invitations the first thing on arriving home. We have a million plans made already, so you can tell your friends to be prepared for two very fresh greenhorns.

And thanks a million.
Mary

Hotel Wellington
Seventh Avenue
Fifty-Fifth and Fifty-Sixth Streets
New York

Mar 15, 1938
N.Y.C.

Dear Mary,

Received your most enjoyable letter. I am pleased to hear you were away as you were getting away. I am answering your letter immediately to let you know that I have arranged for you and Sara to stay that week-end. I have written to Edgar Patience because I'm in hope of him driving down.

Do not worry about any expenses regardless of who you come with. I sent invitations to Mr. & Mrs. Edgar Patience, Mr. & Mrs. Wilmer Patience, Mr. & Mrs. Griffen Reynolds, Buddy & William Grimes and Lois Brown. Make up a party and let me know as soon as you can how many and who is coming. You won't need an invitation so you can give it to someone who would like to come but someone within reason you understand.

Thank your Mother and Father. I'll be busy from now until then so please keep in contact with me.

Thanks for the card. It was nice to be remembered in your excitement. I'll be very anxious to hear from you.

"Luke"

The Letters

March 19, 1938

Dear Luther,

You can't imagine how happy I was to receive your letter. We'll love staying over the weekend. It was grand of you to arrange it for us and we are ever so grateful.

It seems as if everyone in town is planning on going to the dance. The boys over at the hotel are having a royal battle about who is supposed to get off. Even my brother wants to attend, but I told him he is still damp behind the ears and he'd better wait.

It was nice of you to write to Edgar. I appreciate it very much, but please don't go to too much trouble just for our sakes, Luther because we'll be there if we have to hike. But it won't be necessary so don't worry.

I'll write later concerning any details, as I am not so sure about some things myself.

Mary

According to a New York times article published June 6, 2004, Sugar Hill was a ritzy Manhattan neighborhood for the Black bourgeoisie beginning in the 1920s. It was defined by 155th Street to the north, 145th Street to the south, Edgecombe Avenue to the east, and Amsterdam Avenue to the west. It gained its name because it was reflective of money and the 'sweet life.' The neighborhood even has a swimming pool!

When this letter was written, Joe Louis was the world heavy-weight boxing champion.

The dancing Nicholas Brothers (Fayard and Harold)) were huge stars of stage and screen in the 1930's. In 1937, they appeared on Broadway in the Rogers and Hart musical Babes in Arms. They returned "home" in 1938 to Harlem's Cotton Club and remained there until going to Hollywood in 1940.

Mar. 23, 1938
N.Y.C.
Dear Mary,

I heard from Buddy Grimes and said he would bring you and Sarah to this fine affair of the Paragon Club. I'll make the most possible effort to entertain you while you are down here. I regret that everyone in town can't attend the dance but thankful for you and others.

You will stay with my cousin Emily. You will live on what is called Sugar Hill. All the swells live up there. Joe Louis when he's in N.Y. The Nicholas Brothers and others. So don't go high hat on me now.

I suppose the N.Y. Downey's will be there and other Wilkes-Barreans and hundreds of others. Well more next time. Answer soon.
"Luke"
P.S. By the way Sonny will live in the same apt. with you. I wish you well.

The Letters

Hotel Redington
<u>Absolutely Fireproof</u>
Wilkes-Barre, PA.

March 29, 1938

Dear Luther,

   Do you recognize the stationary? You can just about guess what I am doing. The Baums again.* Everyone here has asked me to give you their best regards etc. So you see you are still a big shot. By the way I'm jealous. Helen Louise has told me a big story about your being her first boyfriend. I hope you are properly elated.

   Has Buddy written you that he intends to leave here about 3:30? Goodness, I hope I can stay awake for the next two days. I don't want to be like Harry Brown, sleep all the while I am there.

   Please tell Emily that we appreciate very much her allowing us to stay at her home and don't worry about Sonny, we'll take care of him.

Mary

P.S.

Almost forgot. Chris was here Sunday and Sara wasn't home. She was very sorry though when I told her. He said he'd love to be in N.Y. while we were there. He was in Philadelphia while we were.

M.E.B.

*I believe the Baums were a single mother with a small child who lived in the Hotel Redington and for whom my mother often babysat.

April 5, 1938

Dear Luther,

We'll never be able to thank you enough for the perfectly grand time we had in N.Y. I really loved every minute of it, but I hope I can act more grown up the next time I come.

We told my mother about everything that happened. She and Dad are as excited as we were about the trip. Sara wasn't home five minutes until she'd told them about all my downfalls, even Emily's wine. I had to explain to them about the wine so they wouldn't think I was getting fresh because I was in N.Y. They laughed and laughed at everything we told them. They were as disgusted as we were about Florence and they felt sorry for Buddy.

We got home about eleven fifteen Sunday nite and were we tired. I am still trying to catch up on some rest. We had company last nite and so we had to stay up late again. But not tonite, I don't care if the President comes.

Brother wanted to know if we saw the Milky Way (the Great White Way), the Riviera (France) and heaven knows what else. We told him to study astronomy and geography and he nearly died. He was mortified. Being so dumb and him a Brooks!

After I saw all the nice girls in N.Y., Luther, I really felt that I should begin to worry where I come into the picture. I wish you would have gone to a smaller town. Maybe I could rest a little easier. I hate to admit but I'm afraid I'm jealous.

Mary

Hotel Wellington
Seventh Avenue
Fifty-Fifth and Fifty-Sixth Streets
New York

April 5, 1938

Dear Mr. & Mrs. Brooks,

 I really feel as though I should thank you for giving Mary and Sara the privilege of visiting New York City and being my guests. I tried my very earnest to entertain them to the best of my ability during the short time in which they had to stay.

 They have been and still are being admired by my friends here. I was very pleased and proud of their being here and hope they can make a return visit so I can continue to show them the Wonder City. I'm sure they were not ready to leave when the time came but it was best they did so they could return next time.

 Again, I say thank you and loads of luck to you and the family.

"Luke"

Hotel Wellington
Seventh Avenue
Fifty-Fifth and Fifty-Sixth Streets

April 9, 1938
New York
N.Y.C.

Dear Mary,

The pleasure of having you to entertain is worth more to me than all of the fame that "Lindy" has. I'm really pleased to know that you enjoyed yourself while you were here. I feel as though I've been successful in my achievement.

It was nice of your Mother and Dad to laugh at your doings. I'm only sorry I couldn't show you more of N.Y. but your time was too short. I hope you can come down soon again…it was swell having you here. I admit there are several nice girls I've met since I've been here but who said you weren't nice. There is always a nicest one and that one is Y-O-U!

John wants to come to the dance in Scranton. Let me know when it is. John admires Sara quite a bit also. You bet I let him know that you are mine and to nix off. Jocelyn was pleased to hear from you and she will answer your letter soon.

I think of you when they play 'Marie" at any time. Let's make it our song.

"Luke"

The Letters

April 16, '38

Dear Luther,

I received your very nice letter with loads of appreciation. It seems like two years instead of two weeks since we've been in N.Y. Buddy Grimes has been here several times to talk over the trip. He was embarrassed all the time we were there because we had to wait so much for him and Florence. Also because they had to spend so much time eating. Sara and I have both told him to forget it, as we still had a grand time.

I told your Mother what a good time we had, also how stout you are getting. But that you are still nice to look at and that you haven't changed in any other respect. I wonder how Mothers can think of so many questions in a few minutes. Your mother certainly runs a close second to mine with questions per minute.

I have been very busy since we've come home and I haven't had time to tell Mary Buster about the trip but she is dying to hear all about it. I may have time to tell her next week-end. End her curiosity a little.

Say hello to Winfields, Emily and Sonny for me and give them my very best regards.

I think "Marie" is a very lovely song, too.

Mary

Hotel Wellington
Seventh Avenue
Fifty-Fifth and Fifty-Sixth Streets
New York

April 21, 1938
N.Y.C.
Dear Mary,

Your encouraging remarks were received gratefully. Jocelyn said she was still thinking of you all and would write soon.

Blame yourself because thoughts of your being here still linger with me and I'm not trying to forget. You're so easy to remember and so hard to forget.

I still manage to meet someone from W-B. I heard Chink was in town.

Mothers are that way. Thanks so much for telling her you saw me and also for the nice things you said.

I've been very busy also, working and getting a certain amount of recreation trying to keep fit.

Please tell your mother I really enjoyed her sweet letter. I relayed the welcome remarks to the persons she mentioned and they also were very pleased to hear from her, also my friend Sara and last but not least Mr. Brooks for his remarks.

I did manage to hear Jimmy Lunceford and the show was very good. I met one of the Cotton Club boys the other day and he said Cab was in Wilkes-Barre that night (Wed.).

Well, Mary, the weather is becoming fit and it will make it easier for us to see each other more often.

So until I hear from you again this is
Luke

The Letters

Wilkes-Barre, Pa
April 26, 1938
Dear Luther,

I enjoyed your letter too, and it was nice knowing you still remember my having been there. I don't want you to forget easily anything about me. Remember that, please.

Since spring is here to stay I have been socializing myself. There have been several dances here since Easter. We were to G.A.R. last night to a dance. It was very nice for such a poor school I will admit.

But I have my troubles, Louise and her mother are moving to Newark, N.J. in May and Mary Buster is going back to Kentucky. Louise has definitely broken her engagement. I guess the "love bug" didn't bite hard enough.

Sara and I will have to form a society of our own to keep each other company after everyone is gone.

By the way, we missed having the Wrights home for Easter. They're slipping—it's the first holiday they've ever missed. How are they?

Tell Johnny there will not be any Matron's dance this year. The ladies can't get it together somehow. But the Esquire is giving one sometime later and maybe you can bring him to that.

Give my regards to Jocelyn and him and tell her we're still waiting for that letter.
Mary
I'm late for work—excuse the writing.

May 3, 1938
N.Y.C.

Dear Mary:

So sorry I haven't written soon but I just didn't find time but thinking of it rather strongly.

I heard from my mother today and she tells me your mother is ill, sorry to hear that and I hope she recovers soon.

Gee, you and Sara will be castaways soon. You'll have to be discovered. What has come over Mary that she wants to return to Kentucky? I bet she has become homesick. Louise breaking her engagement I can't seem to understand.

I probably have learned quite a bit but I still say you don't know a fine school when you see it or else you know it but won't acknowledge it. I will not let my alma mater down.

Jocelyn was glad to hear from you, also the others. Well there isn't anything else to say but keep cool.

"Luke"

May 9, 1938

Dear Luther,

As usual I am very busy now that my mother is in the hospital. Sara and I have to keep house and it certainly is a job. It seems we are never thru. We have company every nite. A couple of times I went to sleep while they were here. They'll be calling me "eleven o'clock" Mary again if I don't get over it soon. I think it must be the environment. Too much of the same thing! Sometimes there are six fellows here at a time, all talking at once. I try to be attentive but it doesn't work, I only get sleepy, alas.

I burned my wrist last Monday and so poor Sara had the brunt of the work put on her. I dropped the electric iron on it if you can imagine anything so silly. I'm am awful dope. But I hope it will be better this week so I can take the bandages off and do the million things I have waiting for my special attention.

By the way the Matron's are having their dance the last of this month. They've gotten over their quarrel, sweet things. Also Wash is home to help his Mother move although I haven't seen him yet. Mary Buster is all a flutter.

Well that's all for this time.

Mary

May 13, 1938
N.Y.C.
Dear Mary,

I regret you mother's illness very much. Please remember me to her and I sincerely hope she recovers soon. Please don't work too much. You may strain yourself but I'm so sure that it won't happen.

Emily was robbed last week. She and Mrs. Moore and her daughter were in the house at the time. They were jabbering in the kitchen didn't even hear the unwanted intruder helping himself in the bedroom. He took Mr. Busch's suits and sixteen dollars in cash and a few small articles. Sonny was dead asleep in the same room. You talkative women!

Well Mary, I have moved to my summer residence. You know how it is—one place becomes a bore all the year around. I live on the same street as my cousin lives. I now reside at 261 Edgecombe Ave. It is a private house and I [have] a skylight room. Just a small house like room. I moved last Friday. I went down to Winfield's on Wednesday and found your letter there.

I'm very pleased to hear that you still maintain your overwhelming personality. I just know you become bored, most popular people do.

I hope your infections heal soon so that you can do your share of the housework. Tell Wash to let an old friend hear from him when he has a little spare time.

By the way, that stationary you use comes on like "Gang Busters".*
It really is nice to hear from you.
"Luke"

*My mother's recent letters were written on pink paper.

The Letters

May 20, 1938

Dear Luther,

I want to write first of all, how sorry I am about that terrible stationary. I was afraid you might get more than "Gang Bustered." But it was all we happened to have at the time. I promise it won't happen again.

I was very sorry to read of Emily's misfortune. But please don't think all women are so talkative, we do have our quiet moments of meditation, I assure you.

Also, you're more hard to keep track of than my last week's wages. You're really "worser" than a roving cowboy, I swear. I don't see why you should have been bored. Please try to stand this place because if you move again it will probably be in China some place.

I haven't been overworked as yet but we are terribly busy. I go to see my mother every day. She has really been quite ill, but I think she is starting to get well now. They have taken all her teeth out. As soon as her heart is more improved they are going to take her tonsils out. She strained her heart pretty bad coughing so they make her stay in bed all the time. But she'll be as good as ever soon, I hope.

Mary

May 27, 1938
N.Y.C.

Dear Mary,

Charmed to hear from you. The apology for your stationary was unnecessary. It was quite fascinating. Send some more if you have it.

I heard that Mrs. Haley, my aunt is here. Well I suppose I'll have to see her and let her tell me some of the news from home. Everyone has the same line of speech for the old burg.

I think I'll be here for a while. You know I'm a believer of that old, ancient adage which readeth thusly: a rolling stone gathers no moss. So don't be surprised if you hear of me in another part of the world. That's one way I differ from the rest of the Snyders. You'll always know where I am regardless of where I go.

I've been away from Wilkes-Barre one year this past Thursday (May 26). Do you remember, Buddy, Sara, you and me took a ride in Buddy's car the night before I left or do you remember, but I have been home a week-end since? Do you remember?

I sincerely hope for your mother's recovery and good health, I really do. I know the rest of the family misses her as they should but I'm sure they will make up for it on the return of your charming mother. My regards to her.

Well cheerio until next time.

"Luke"

The Letters

June 3, 1938

Dear Luther,

I enjoyed your missive to the utmost. It was "delovely" knowing you still remembered our parting. But, Luther, I hope you weren't bragging of you having been only home once in a year. Weren't you homesick just once in all that long year?

Also, don't refer to Wilkes-Barre as the "old burg"—after all it's still your home town.

If you see Mrs. Haley, tell her everything is O.K. Mr. Haley put out a very nice laundry last week. If she stays a little longer he'll be ready to go into business.

My "charming" mother (and you can be sure she appreciated that) had her tonsils removed this afternoon. And without anesthetic! The cocaine has just about driven her nuts, it is very painful.* But now she comes home in a few days, she hopes, and you'll hear my shouts of joy all the way to N.Y.

Well, Luther, until next time, cheers.

Mary

P.S. Sorry we haven't any more of that ultra-smart stationary. Glad you did like it though!

M.E.B.

*There is a history of cocaine being used as a medical anesthetic. According to the American Academy of Otolaryngology, no other drug combines the anesthetic and vasoconstricting properties of cocaine.

Hotel Wellington
Seventh Avenue
Fifth-Fifth and Fifty-Sixth Streets
New York

June 10, 1938
N.Y.C.

Dear Mary:

Yours was received and read and reread. I must heartily thank you for a year of very interesting letter receiving. I enjoyed every letter of each word, every word of each sentence, every sentence of each paragraph of each correspondence. Your letters have been a consolation since I've been away and I've looked forward to receiving them with great expectations. Please continue. I'm taking inventory. I calculated that I've received ninety-eight letters which is an average of two a week.* Thanks to you Mary.

It was swell news to hear of your mother and I'm sure she will be around as she was before. My thoughts are with her. Mrs. Haley asked about her. She was also pleased to hear of her better half's ambition.

The swimming pool is very convenient from where I live. When you come down next week, or I mean next time, we'll go in. Don't forget your bathing suit—or perhaps your skates according to the weather when you arrive. Are you going to play tennis this summer? My tennis racket is up there. I may send for it. I'll have a lot of time for sport because we are not working very much. Things have gotten slow. I already started to become very colored again from old man Sol.

I still proclaim my hobby of keeping a scrapbook or two. One of them contains "Believe it Or Not" and the wise sayings of Chink Chow. The other contains social scraps.

I saw Maude Roche. She lives but a few doors from me. She is a married lady now—so help me. I also saw Ben Johnson at the La Marcheri. Do your remember La Marcheri?

I suppose that is enough for this time. I see you or I mean I'll hear from you later.

Just "Luke"

My father's arithmetic is a bit off. He received about two letters per month, not two per week.

June 17, 1938

Dear Luther,

Your very sweet missive was received with the utmost appreciation. It's been a great pleasure this year receiving your letters and every one has been enjoyed, as you must know.

Today I've done nothing but bid my friends fare-well. Louise, Mary B. and Dorothy Walker all leave this week-end. Louise was in Scranton for three weeks but they leave tomorrow morning for Newark. Mary goes back to Kentucky and Dorothy to Ala. School left out today and they are not losing a moment in getting away. Poor Mary is still a sophomore. They've become very attached to her and don't want to part. My sister is a senior. You know, it makes me feel grown-up knowing that she is growing up.*

Sara and I have been very busy. Trying to hold down jobs and keep house at the same time. I mean it's wearing us down. I work every day including Sunday. Thank heavens it's not house work. A month of nice work has helped me settle my nerves and get rid of my jitters.

Luther, I don't know about bringing my bathing suit. It's a terrific let down for me. I look like twelve in one. But I'll eat lots of spinach and maybe that will help. I hope!

So until the next time, Bon Jour.

Mary

Mary was referring to her youngest sibling, Lillian. In several letters she's simply referred to as 'Sister.'

The Letters

On June 19, 1936 boxer Joe Louis fought German boxer Max Schmeling, the underdog. To the surprise of all, Schmeling defeated Louis, a loss that would continue to sting long after the match ended. In 1937, Louis defeated world heavyweight champion James J. Braddock in Chicago to become the new world champ. However, according to Louis's official website, he stated, "I don't want nobody to call me champ until I beat Max Schmeling." My father's letter refers to the June 22nd rematch between Schmeling and Louis.

Hotel Wellington
Seventh Avenue
Fifty-Fifth and Fifty-Sixth Streets
New York

June 27, 1938
N.Y.C.

Dear Mary,

Please excuse this long delay but within the last week I've been interviewed and tried out and the result your boyfriend is now a bellman in the Hotel Taft, a larger and even better hotel than the Wellington. I hope that I can stay here for a while, don't you?

Nice to hear of your sister's advancement in school. Please congratulate her for me.

I suppose you were elated over Joe Louis' hasty victory of Der Max. I wish you could have seen Harlem that night. No traffic was allowed to pass through Seventh Avenue or Lenox Avenue. They simply went wild.

I've been in the pool twice so far. Saturday, the spooks were in the pool eight deep. You couldn't swim or dive but it was fun.

I suppose you've talked to Mrs. Haley. I guess Sonny will be down there soon.

Well I guess there isn't any other trash to tell you so keep sweet.
"Luke"

Dolly Dawn, was a well-known vocalist in the late 1930's and '40s. She was a member of the George Hall's Hotel Taft Orchestra and appeared daily on radio broadcasts from the Taft's Grill Room. When she died in 2002, her obituary published December 18 in 'The New York Times' stated she was the first vocalist to become the sole focus of a band at a time when the musicians were typically the main draw.

July 4, 1938
Dear Luther,

It was nice hearing from you once again. I know you must be proud of working in a big hotel such as the Taft. I do hope you stay there a very long time. Don't forget to listen to Dolly Dawn for me if she is still there. I'll think of you when I hear her.

Emily and Sonny are here. Sonny was here only a few minutes when he had a host of admirers watching him while he proceeded to [entertain] our guests, the McBride kids from Catawissa. He even tried taking up our sidewalks but Emily halted him then. What a man!

Art Sands is home. Louise has an adorable baby girl. My friend Mrs. King had a big son but he died after six hours, poor thing. Also Harriet Dennis has a daughter. So you see your home town is still progressing in some ways.

This is the most terrible holiday I've ever spent. This whole family has gone away. My mother, ill enough to be in bed, has taken Brother and Sister to Scranton. Sara and Dad are working at the Fox Hill Country Club. Poor me had to fill in for Sara at the theater. I'm her extra now, you know, besides my own job. I had to get my own supper and invite Evelyn Payne over to eat with me. I hate to eat alone. I think it's terrible but what can I do?
Mary

The Letters

Hotel Taft
7th Ave. at 50th St.
New York

July 9, 1938
N.Y.C.
Dear Mary,

    Your cheerful letter was received and welcomed as usual.

    So far working has been O.K. I let Dolly, George Hall and the boys have the summer off so I engaged Enoch Light's Orchestra for the summer. Fun but the day I started to work Dolly said to me it's no use for us both to be here so I let her go for the summer. I'm just that way. But you've got to think of me before you hear her again.

    I guess Sonny is the talk of that part of State. St. and thereabouts. My mother will be down here Monday—that's a break, I've got to take her around to the hot spots.

    I ate dinner with Ben Johnson the Friday before the fourth of July and he said he would be in Wilkes-Barre on the Fourth and he was going to drop by your house but you being so busy that day maybe you weren't home when he called.

    Who did I see parading past the hotel one day but George and Chris as proud as peacocks. They work in New Jersey. Chris asked about you and Sara. Tell Art I said he was a big stooge because he didn't come back.

    It looks as though some of the folks are trying hard to replace those who have left. Wilkes-Barre—well more power to them.

    I had a lot of fun at the pool the other day. Don Redman was there and some other celebrities. They had a beauty contest and took pictures.

    Tell me Mary, do you think you'll be down anytime this summer? As ever,
"Luke"

July 17, 1938

Dear Luther,

It was grand hearing from you again. I really enjoyed reading every word.

I know you had a gala time entertaining your mother. I was surprised when on my way home from work, I ran into her on Main Street. She seems to have enjoyed herself very much.

Florence Roach was telling us about Maude going to the same pool where you attend. Did you ever see her? Also, if you see Chris, give him our regards, please.

We are rather looking forward to the picnic this year. They are planning a large dance this year. With so many new people in the Poconos they think it will be a success. There are really some nice people up there this year. We have met some nice fellows. There are also some nice people who come from N.J. quite often. They intend to be here too.

Poor Art is still here and he really is very lonesome. I really feel sorry for him.

Luther, I don't know whether I'll get to N.Y. this summer or not. I surely would love to come you know that, but I don't know how I can arrange it. My mother is still pretty ill, but on the road to recovery so that will help. Also, I get no vacation so far. We've just gotten a new boss.

But here's hoping.

Mary

The Letters

July 25, 1938
N.Y.C.
Dear Mary,

So glad to hear from you again but that isn't news.

My mother wrote me and she mentioned your meeting her on Main St. By the way, what part of W-B is that street in?

Florence, or rather Maude Roach, goes swimming by sight not action, so you can relay that to Florence.

I sincerely hope that you have the utmost enjoyment at the picnic. Regardless of how much you have you really deserve more. I'll be with you that day in mind but not in body.

Sorry you can't be down here on the 29th the day after the picnic because there is a moonlight boat ride that night sponsored by the Y.M.C.A.

Well Mary, whenever you can come down, it will be a pleasure to entertain you. Always keep that in mind. I hope your mother recovers one hundred percent.

Tell Sonny I said "Hello" and all my friends at the picnic. Please write and tell me about it.

"Luke"

Aug. 1, 1938

Dear Luther,

I wonder how many times I've written "Dear Luther." But it's still a pleasure, I could write it forever as long as you care to read it.

It's been so hot here. I'm about to join a nudist cult, only I'm too modest, woe is me. And I'm as shady as any of your people could hope to be, darn sun.

Luther, I must tell you about my new boss. She is from N.Y. and she's a regular killer. She is very friendly and does she know N.Y. Maybe that is why I like her so well. Also, she has a boyfriend at the Hotel Clinton. Is that near yours? By the way a couple of the clerks here intend to vacation in N.Y. They usually stay at the Taft. If they do this time, they are going to ask for you. I told them how marvelous you are, such a big shot. Thank you.

The picnic was terrible but the dance was colossal. The new pavilion is really beautiful. There was a nice crowd also, but the darn thing ended too soon as usual.

Howard was home. Olin and Tommy returned from California also.

If I've missed any news it wasn't because I didn't try. Almost forgot—do you see much change from the last one?

Mary

The Letters

Hotel Taft
7th Ave. and 50th St.
New York

Aug. 7, 1938
N.Y.C.
Dear Mary:

Your letters are still as sweet as the very first one I received from you. In fact, you've added a certain something to them.

As for the temperature, I am in sympathy with you. Keeping cool is a popular hardship down here. But don't give up—cooler days are coming.

I can depend on you to give our praising words of me to someone—and believe me you can depend on the same from me for you.

I think the hotel you were referring to is downtown from my hotel. Thanks so much for your very kind words of me. All I've got to do now is live up to them. It's sweet to know you enjoyed the picnic and dance. Olin and Tommy seem to have done a bit of traveling, swell. I hope to go there someday myself. I wish I could have seen Howard. Does he still talk as much?

Your picture was just tutty-fruity. I showed it to Jocelyn and she said you look younger on it than the others. My opinion is that it is charming and I'll treasure it. You're just a dear on a deer, now ain't that somethin'.

Well try to keep cool and I'm sure you'll keep sweet.
"Luke"

Aug. 12, 1938

Dear Luther,

It was really a pleasure to receive your latest. I enjoyed it very much, thank you.

I'm glad you liked the snapshot. I've had a birthday since that was taken. Sorry it didn't show the advancement in my age. I'm disappointed, really.

Sara was almost in N.Y. last week-end. But after packing and getting up at an un Godly hour she changed her mind. Rudy and Eldra were really disappointed. But they hope to go again soon.

Chris and Andy are home for a few days. They are very busy hunting up some excitement. Poor fellows, I'm afraid it's hopeless.

Tell Emily Sonny is having the time of his life. He comes over about every nite for supper and stays until bedtime. He does everything and tries to say everything. All I can understand is "please".

You'll have to excuse the writing. There are a gang of kids here and I'm nearly goofy, the crazy things. Rudy and I were singing duets—maybe that's what's wrong.

Until the next time.

Mary

Hotel Taft
7th Ave. and 50th St.
New York

Aug. 19, 1938
N.Y.C.
Dear Mary,

Your swell and appreciated letter was more than welcome. Let me congratulate you on having another birthday and may you live to be [blessed] with many more. As you grow older you improve your glamour.

Sonny was welcomed home. Also, Mrs. Haley returned.

I saw Chris the other day but he was in a hurry and I didn't have a chance to talk to him about hometown. I suppose he'll have the same old story.

Look here, you must turn those kids out when you write a letter. They can't do that to you. You mean you were singing a solo unless Rudy improved his vocal ability because he was very rank when I heard him trying to sing last.

There really isn't anything more to say so I'll be waiting for your answer.

"Luke"

P.S. Please remember me to your mother and the rest of the family.

Aug. 26, 1938

Dear Luther,

I really enjoyed hearing from you. Nice to know Mrs. Haley and Sonny arrived safely. They had such a hard time starting. Give my regards to all of them.

There is really nothing to write about for once. I am at a loss for words. This place really gets one down at times.

We do have a new theater "Comerford." Celebrated Comerford week in its honor. "Hicksville."

The girls in our store call it "shanty-town" and I agree heartily.

Please forgive this short letter. I'll try to do better next time.

Mary

The Letters

Hotel Taft
7th Ave. and 50th St.
New York

Aug. 30, 1938
N.Y.C.
Dear Mary:

I received your short but welcome letter. I expect to receive a long letter each and every time I hear from you but the shortest and the longest are all very much appreciated.

They really are building up the old town, aren't they? In just about one hundred years it will be as large as Harlem. I suppose when I come home I'll have to have a guide to take [me] around. There I go dreaming again.

Sonny and Mrs. Haley were glad to hear from you. Remember me to the family.

We, the Taft men, will hold our dance on Sat. Oct 8, 1938 so start to prepare for this occasion. The invitations aren't printed yet but as soon as we receive them I'll send some to you and your friends. The dance will be semi-formal this year.

It seems as though the summer is over already because it has turned rather cool within the last few days. It has stopped the swimmers and beach-goers.

Well my little friend, until the next time, may I rest my pen and wait for your answer.
"Luke"

Sept. 4, 1938

Luther, dear,

I just thought I'd try a little variation in the salutations. Don't you think its cute?

Your very delightful letter was much appreciated and I am thinking of Oct. 8 with the <u>utmost</u> pleasure, please believe me.

You could never guess whom we've been entertaining. He is not famous or renown so I'll tell you as you'd never guess. A bartender from the Savoy Ballroom. Maude Roach brought him here when she came home. He is really very nice. Edgar Phipps is his name by the way. (I was listening to a song and scribbled. Sorry.)

Fancy us with a bartender. There was a Bill somebody too. I don't recall his name.

Well, my N.Y. boss has left, and am I sorry. She was fun and she loved talking about the "Big City." But the girls keep repeating things she said and we are all homesick for the place.

By the way, my brother has a driver's license and he wants to drive us to N.Y. But I told him to stick to small towns for a while for safety's sake.

So now I'll wait until you answer.

Mary

Hotel Taft
7th Ave. and 50th St.
New York

Sept. 10, 1938
N.Y.C.
Dear Mary,

Nice knowing you are well and very grateful for the salutation. You know any salutation is well accepted whether it be written, verbal or action, the latter preferable.

Glad to hear that I can look forward to you being in the City once again. You can tell your friends that any one can attend this dance. They do not need invitations although I will send some down there. The dance is informal and the admission is one dollar. We have been planning a very fine function and I assure you that who ever makes the trip here will not be sorry unless it is Miss Glover.

I saw Maude the very same day I received your letter and she told me she had a friend up there with her. I don't know that bartender. I say that a bartender is just the worst person you could be with.

Your brother has accomplished the art of driving a car—well say he also can operate the vehicle. I under-rated his skill so he is to be congratulated.

Well my little friend, I hope who ever comes down will bring you with them and let me know before Oct 8th just who is coming.

So until next time.
"Luke"

Sept. 19, 1938
Dear Luther,

I am sorry for the delay in answering your very delightful letter, but I have truly been busy. My mother is very, very ill again in the hospital and our relatives have been literally camping here. Our house is in a constant uproar all the time any more. I hardly know whether I'm coming or going.

We received your invitations, also, and thank you very much for sending them. I don't know whether we will get to N.Y. now or not. At present it seems very doubtful. We are really disappointed but it cannot be helped.

Your cousin Paul had an accident. He was hit by a car and spent several days in the hospital. But he is out now—hail and hardy and just as pesty.

Since there really isn't any news to interest the most interested, I'll close until next time.

Mary

The Letters

Hotel Taft
7th Ave. and 50th St.
New York

Sept. 23, 1938
N.Y.C.
Dear Mary:

I really regret hearing of your Mother's illness. I do hope she recovers soon. You all have my deepest sympathy. She has to recover, I'm sure. Don't you excite yourself too much or you will break down. Try and take it as easily as possible.

I heard of Paul's accident but I suppose he has completely recuperated, I hope.

Gee, you not attending the dance is a very disappointing, really it is. We've gotten the dance talked up pretty well from downtown to the Bronx through Harlem and up on the Hill. We got a powerful advertising system. I hope that someone from down there comes up because I sort of told the boys about you all. They are trying to get some news for the paper but I ain't saying too much, you know I ain't talkin'.

Well, if you can't come this time there will be more later but ours is the best, you know. I've got to say so because that is the old Taft spirit. Well I hope you all will survive all right so until next time.
"Luke"

Oct. 4, 1938

Dear Luther,

After reading your very nice letter, I really feel I shall miss your affair very much. Quite a few people here are planning on going. It remains to be seen how many attend, although I don't think you will be disappointed.

My mother is still very ill and we have been kept <u>very</u> busy. I hope they help her this time because I feel about ready to join her.

Florence Roach tells me her sister has gone housekeeping for herself, only she is afraid to stay in her apartment alone. Don't tell me it's that bad in N.Y. I'd hate to be disillusioned, really I would.

Please sit out one dance for me. I'll be thinking of it all Saturday.

Mary

Hotel Taft
7th Ave. and 50th St.
New York

N.Y.C.

10-10-38

Dear Mary:

 I hope your mother recovers soon—also keep yourself well. So sorry you couldn't attend the dance but I'm so sure you would have.

 I am very much disappointed with the home folks. Not one of them were present. Not even those that live down here except Charley Downey. The dance was colossal. We balled too long. That's what I'm talking about. I suppose you don't understand those expressions, but in plain English, we had a h____ of a good time.

 I hope that next time you can be present so that you can retrieve what you have missed, but what is the matter with the homeys—have they gotten antique. You can tell them for me that they are my idea of a pain in the place where you can't put plaster personified. I mean it too. I'll come up and tell them myself.

 Well, my little friend, I sincerely hope you have better news for me when you answer my letter so until then, keep up the old fight and bear down.

"Luke"

Oct. 16, 1938

Dear Luther,

It was nice hearing from you. But I was sorry to read that you were so very disappointed. You can be sure I have relayed your remarks with the proper emphasis. Buddy, Rudy, Gene Moore, and others really did intend to go but circumstances prevented some and others didn't care to go alone, unfortunately.

So please don't hold it against them. They are planning on coming to N.Y. some Saturday nite for Sunday and having a <u>hard</u> time. Maybe then you can show all of what we missed last time.

My mother came home last Sunday afternoon, surprising us all. But she is still far from well although she has improved. She and Brother have gone to my cousin's for a while so she can recuperate further.

Your mother has called often and we certainly appreciate it. She is really very sweet and you may tell her so.

I'm going to close now and listen to George Hall and Dolly Dawn, my favorites for the moment.

Mary

The Letters

Hotel Taft
7th Ave. and 50th St.
New York

Oct. 24, 1938
N.Y.C
Dear Mary:

After reading your gracious letter I think it fitting and proper to respond. Although I was quite disappointed because of your not arriving in the city for our dance, now it has become a thing of the past and I think just as much of you all again.

It was very welcome news to hear of your mother's homecoming. I really hope she can stay home and regain her normal self. My mother also told me she made a visit to your home and I think it was very charming or somethin'.

It will be very nice if you come down on a Saturday or Sunday—still better on a Friday because that is my day off. If Sara comes tell her I have a nice boyfriend for her. I have showed him the pictures. There will be quite a few fine affairs this winter. While I'm sure you can't attend all of them, you perhaps can make one or two. Hip my friend Edgar about it also. I suppose he still is a married man.

Well my little friend, I suppose there isn't anything more so I'll say solong until the next time.

"Luke"

Oct. 31, 1938

Dear Luther,

I was glad you found it, or rather still find it proper to answer my little missives such as they are. Being a proper person myself I wouldn't care for anything improper, if you can get what I mean.

Also, I do not like that "my little friend" jive. I much rather "toots" if it must be anything, although there are a few who still find <u>Mary</u> a nice name. So in the future please refrain from nicknames.

I was sorry to read you still feel disappointed over the "homeys" not attending your affair. But you were not nearly as disappointed as we were, remember that.

One of the girls from our own store, a cute little redhead spent the week-end in N.Y. She and her friend stopped off at your hotel. She waited to see you but that you were all so busy she couldn't make a special request for services and so she omitted them altogether.

By the way, Edgar P. is still married so far as I know. I don't see or hear of him very much.

Adios until the next time.

Excuse the rush please,

Mary

Hotel Taft
7th Ave. and 50th St.
New York

Nov. 7, 1938
N.Y.C.
Toots Dear:

All you need now is a Casper and a little Butter Cup and you'll knock yourself right-out, you really will.

I hope that all of you are making it O.K.

If I were asked for at the hotel, they would have to ask for my number which happens to be seven. Then again my other names are Specs, Freckles and Frec. It seems as though I have entirely abandoned my true name.

Homeys are the only ones that call me my true name. I forgot I had freckles until I came to N.Y., but really I don't mind.

I have heard that your alma mater hasn't lost a football game this season. Perhaps I really didn't want to mention it but I'm just a good sport. Every team has its lucky year, so I reckon it's your dear Coughlin's year. I don't think you would of told me if G.A.R. were victorious this year. Are you going to see Coughlin play Kingston Thanksgiving morning? Perhaps your old school spirit has decreased now that you have become a lady in full.

Nothing more except I'll see that your orders are carried out My Little Friend.

"Luke"

Nov. 15, 1938
Dear Luther,

You see I'm being very nice in remembering you have a good Christian name; but we don't forget your freckles, they being so obvious.

Must you persist in calling me your little friend? Other people consider me quite grown up and sophisticated, ahem! We were in Binghamton to a dance last nite and not once was I referred to as a "chick" or a "chippy," so there. And we really had a very lovely evening—it couldn't have been nicer except maybe if you were there. I always have admired your dancing, you know.

It was really very nice of you to mention the triumphs of my alma mater. I'd have done the same only your "almer" has done so poorly that I really felt that silence in that direction was kinder in every way. I intended to go to the game on Thanksgiving, but it seems to be getting colder and colder and I've changed my mind. Andy wanted us to come to Washington for the Lincoln—Howard game but Washington is a little too far for a one day trip. So we'll be contented with home fires and such, as usual.

By the way, it would take more than a Casper and Butter Cup to knock me out, 'cause I'm a strong woman.

<u>Big Mary</u>
Sara says hold everything, she'll be there.

Hotel Taft
7th Ave. and 50th St.
New York

Nov. 22, 1938
N.Y.C.
Dear Mary:

It's very nice for you to go places but I'm going to jump as salty as a mackerel if I hear you are going any place for a day or two and not coming down here. What are you going to make out of life? Binghamton used to be my old stomping ground. Are you taking up where I left off? The reason they didn't call you a "chippy" is because you are strange to those folks in Binghamton, though you know I don't think you're a chippy any more—not much.

I really appreciate your compliment as to my dancing with you and you know that goes double for me to you.

A friend of mine that I work with was planning to attend the football game in Washington but our plans were foiled so therefore we shall also spend our Thanksgiving in dear Old New York.

I was to a dance last Friday and Charley brought his three sisters with him, Rosabelle, Minnie and Katherine. I couldn't imagine him with the family at a dance just like hometown.

Tell Sara I'm trying to hold everything but its getting too hot to handle….

Hurry, Hurry!

A jolly old Thanksgiving to you and the family—eat until you bust.
"Luke"

Nov. 28, 1938

Dear Luther,

Your very sweet letter was received and appreciated.

We spent a very quiet Thanksgiving but we had lots of company in spite of the snow. The kids have just about made this their second home, so help me! Were you surprised at the weather? I certainly was.

We went to a dance Thursday eve and there was a regular gala. The dance was nearly over before my feet even began to thaw out.

Well, Smarty, Coughlin completed a perfect season in football, every game a cinch without even a tie. (You can pat my shoulder later.) G.A.R also completed a perfect season, every game lost, yes <u>every</u> one. Well, better luck next time. I mean season.

Can you imagine someone told my dad that Chris Hillman was contemplating marriage? The hearts that beat for him here will be disappointed. He certainly got around, at least a dozen will suffer, woe is me.

An old friend of yours was here to call. Do you remember Curley Stewart? I believe that is his name. He is from Scranton. I've seen him often at "318" in Scranton. Is that where you met him? Another of your old haunts. So you see we really are taking up where you left off. We go to all the clubs between here, Scranton, and Stroudsburg. We don't waste any time, not us.

And don't forget we always consider N.Y. first when we think of traveling. I love it, I really do.

Mary

Hotel Taft
7th Ave. and 50th St.
New York

Dec. 6, 1938
N.Y.C.
Dear Mary,

Nice to know you still hold your local popularity. There is every reason why you should. If I were there I suppose I would be one of your callers also.

That storm was a killer. I was snowed in. I went to dinner and had to camp at the house all night.

I have some spare time until after the holidays. The management of the Taft said there was not enough business for them, so I'm being laid off until after the first of the year. Perhaps I will work now and then at the Wellington, until I go back to the Taft.

I don't quite remember this Curly Stewart but it seems very hard for me to remember the male sex. So you are an around-the-towner now, be careful.

You don't mean to tell me that they still have dances in W.B. Do they still do the Virginia Reel and the good old Farmer Dance?

Don't forget N.Y. dear.
"Luke"

My mother displays her temper for the first time in one of her letters. It was a life-long attribute of her personality.

Dec. 16, 1938
Dear Luther,

I didn't mean to be so long in answering your little note but I am really very busy. I work late practically every night at the store in the Christmas rush. Our store caters especially to gentleman shoppers and we are simply swamped.

I was astounded to read of all the leisure time allotted you. It just isn't fair when I have to work so much. If ever there are women presidents things will be changed, I hope.

Our friend Mary Buster is back in Scranton, although I haven't seen her yet.

Yes, Mr. Snyder, we do have dances here. The last dance I went to made me so angry I simply swore at Sara's boyfriend, that nasty Foster-boy, and went home. If it weren't for Gene Moore I'd have walked all the way home in the rain, anything to put the "Y" behind me. Sometime, I'm going to burn the place down, really. Sara was embarrassed at my display of temper. But there is a limit to everything and that "Y"; I mean the "S.S.Y." is far exceeding any limit. You see I'm still angry.

By the way the hotel where you made your debut has bought the bell-hops some very gorgeous uniforms, blue and grey. So you see, the Hotel Redington is still going strong, bless it.

Shame on you forgetting your friends. Sara asks if you still remember her. Also, nobody is able to handle her. (She thinks.) <u>She</u> calls me old maid. She says tell your friend that.
Mary

Hotel Taft
7th Ave. and 50th St.
New York

Dec. 20, 1938
N.Y.C.
Dear Mary:

Yours is forgiven, for the delay. Perhaps I'll do the same some day. I used to be busy also, so can sympathize with you.

How do you find the gentleman customers? Easy to please or difficult? I bet much easier than the females.

Listen, I really don't appreciate your anger. It does not fit your charm. Remember this anger disrupts beauty so I do not care to hear when you are in that mood but don't get that way anymore—if you do keep it within yourself. You can't blame the "Y" itself. It is a wonderful organization. Of course this isn't a written speech but it is a fact.

And Sara calling you old maid is beyond because she had all the earmarks of that sort of character when I left W.B. but they do say that time changes things. If this is so, come back to life Mary.

I've made beautiful speeches about you and Sara to my friends so all <u>you've</u> <u>got</u> to do is prove your worth.

Well I wish you and the family oodles of Christmas cheer and keep your nose shiny.

"Luke"

Dec. 28, 1938

Dear Luther,

Now that I am not quite so busy, I'll answer sooner. I do hope that you had as nice a Christmas as we had. I've been celebrating just as hard as I worked the last few weeks. Most of our friends came home for the holidays. Louise, Andy, Ben, and of course Mary Buster. Sara and I helped each to celebrate and we've been kept pretty busy. Even the "homeys" required our presence though the last few days I've just slept everywhere I've been. It's that old habit of mine. It keeps me from being sophisticated.

Was Santa very good to you? He treated us all "royally". Also it was the first holiday this year my mother wasn't ill. And that was everything.

Also, I must tell you how much we appreciate the fine things you say of us all. We'll have a hard time living up to it so please go a little easy and just hold everything.

So until the next time toodle-loo,

Mary

Your card was cute but it did remind me of "my little friend"

1939

Nineteen thirty-nine was the year of the New York World's Fair. Held in the Flushing Meadows area of Queens, it captured the spirit of American optimism and emerging technology. The Radio Corporation of America (RCA) introduced television to the public for the first time at the Fair. As published on 'The RCA Story' web page, Fair visitors got to see television and were given wallet cards to prove they'd been *televised*.

England's King George VI and Queen Mary visited America in 1939. During their visit, the couple visited Washington D.C., New York City and spent two days at President Roosevelt's home at Hyde Park. The FDR Library web page emphasizes the significance of their visit:

> "No reigning British Monarch had ever set foot on American soil, not even in colonial times. Ever since America declared its independence from England in 1776, the United States and Great Britain oftentimes experienced tense relations, but Roosevelt's invitation to the King carried great significance in the history of Anglo-American relations, not only because of their colonial past, but more importantly, because it signified the dawn of a new era in American and British cooperation."

The Letters

Unfortunately, a few months after this visit, the world leaped closer to war when Germany invaded Poland on September 1. Just before dawn, German planes bombed Polish cities, including the capital, Warsaw. Over one million German troops invaded Polish Territory. Immediately, Britain and France mobilized their forces to prepare to wage war on Germany for the second time in the twentieth century.

My father begins the year a bit tipsy and scrawls an emotional message to my mother written at a forty-five degree angle across seven pages of hotel stationary. My mother doesn't take it too seriously! Nineteen thirty-nine, however, is a very serious year for the Brooks family. An unspeakable tragedy occurred that haunted my mother for years and still casts a shadow over members of my extended family.

Hotel Wellington
Seventh Avenue
Fifty-Fifth and Fifty-Sixth Streets
New York

Jan 1, 1939
NYC
Dear Mary,
Happy New Year Baby!

It is now 9 a.m. New Year Year's Day and I just come in from one of those wild New Year's nights and the first and only one I could think about is you and before I retire I must express myself and let you know how I feel.

Well, baby I'm sure you heard of the Empire State Bldg. Well that is definitely the highest building. Well, baby I got that some. I'm sending you a picture and just let you see for yourself. Don't believe me? Look at the picture. Without a doubt Mary you really are sweet. I didn't realize it was Christmas had it not been for you. Your present really touched me deeply. In fact, you make it seem like Christmas ever since I met you. You know, every day is a holiday since the day that I met you—so help me!

Yes indeed, Mary, you really do things to me. Please excuse the writing but the lines on this paper seem a little crooked this morning. They really do but I know you don't mind. You're that sweet little girl you were when I left the *Old Town*. Sometimes I wish I were there but then again, it's nice to be away. It really helped me to enjoy my Christmas knowing you enjoyed yours—also knowing you had such swell company to entertain, and most of all, your charming mother was well too.

The Letters

Well, Mary, let's both hope that before next year we can see each other again and loads of luck to you and the family. Please excuse this missive, baby.

I'll do better next time.
X Luke

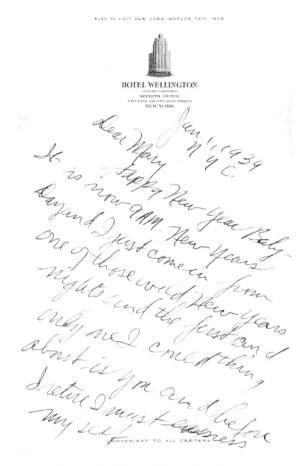

Luther's Happy New Year letter

Jan. 5, 1939
Dear Dizzy,

And aren't you dizzy any more? After reading your letter my eyes could not see anything straight for yours. I was really shocked Luther; but you were really sweet to think of me so early in the morning when you were feeling so good.

Your picture was very enlightening also. I knew then you were really "high."

We were out New Year's Eve also, much to my dismay. Only we managed to get in before dawn, a little after six. I wasn't able to go to work Tuesday, I'm sorry to say but I am catching up with my rest now. All last week I didn't get enough sleep and I guess I just can't take it.

(They're not spots in front of your eyes, it's Sara's pen). Excuse them, please.

Florence Glover got too gay last Saturday and "did that thing." Bud felt very bad when he heard she married Virgil Smith. It was an awful let down, don't you think?

"Doc" Littlepage and his wife are now proud parents of a new daughter.[*] You know of course they live in Oklahoma now. So time still marches on.

And again, thanks for the telegram of good wishes. It was a pleasant surprise and I appreciate your thoughtfulness, I really do.

This letter is a mess, I know, but this is my lunch hour and a very fleeting one so I must hurry.

<u>I am not high.</u>

Mary

**J. Morton Littlepage was a dentist who lived in Wilkes-Barre during the early 1930s.*

The Letters

My father tries to write metaphorically but it doesn't quite work out. One does not reap seeds. They're planted.

Hotel Wellington
Seventh Avenue
Fifty-Fifth and Fifty-Sixth Streets
New York

Jan. 16, 1939
N.Y.C.
Dear Mary:

    I am still dizzy which my last letter proved. After I had mailed the letter I gave myself a darn good laugh. I get that way once in a while but they tell me I am harmless and very amusing so as long as it isn't any more than that I'll try it again sometime. So glad you took it the way you did that helps to prove the former remarks that I have written.

    So you did a bit of celebrating also. I suppose everyone tried to do some that particular night hoping that the coming year reaps better seed than the one just past.

    I will say no more about your freckled letter. Gee, I suppose Buddy was sort of let down about Florence but you can never tell about a lady. The nicer you are to them the faster they lose interest. Perhaps it is the same way with a man. He shouldn't let it bring him down though and be a man and play his cards to win another lady. The world is full of disappointments so he can just record that as another one—poor fellow.

    So "Doc and Mrs. Littlepage had to travel all the way to Oklahoma to have a little brat—didn't like the W-B environment I suppose. Well, lots of luck to them and their offspring.

    Well, my dear, take your time and I hope you all aren't snow bound and hello to the family and your friends.
"Luke"

January 24, 1939

Dear Luther,

How's everything now? I hope everything's under control, because you had me worried, you know. As a rule you don't stray from the straight and narrow, or do you? And besides I don't like to think that I have a dizzy boyfriend, so there.

Now I have another bone to pick with you. Do you realize you have not visited your hometown for, let me see…about sixteen months (I counted on my fingers, so what). And that really isn't very nice. So if you don't give a little thought in that direction soon I'll rebel, and I'm an awful rebeller, too, remember that.

You had your nerve calling the daughter of a former "first citizen" a "brat." I was really shocked.

Now after this very grouchy letter, I close with apologies, but it's just what you need.

Love and Kisses (to take away the bad taste)

Mary

Hotel Wellington
Seventh Avenue
Fifty-Fifth and Fifty-Sixth Streets
New York

Jan 30, 1939*
N.Y.C
Dear Mary,

    I think I am pretty well straightened out now, thanks for asking. I'll try to be just the kind you want me to be from now on.

    I met Jocelyn and her mother and the baby on the avenue and they asked about you and Sarah. Jocelyn also informs me that the dance is on March 10th this year. If it is possible for you and Sarah to come alone do it. If not come with someone whom will not keep you waiting half of the time while you are here. More about that later.

    I often think about coming home for a week-end but that is all the closer I get to home, although as far as my thoughts in that direction, they stay that way. Please do not rebel because I couldn't bear such from you.

    Have you any jitterbugs in W-B? Well if you haven't, I think we can spare you a few and will not miss them. I was down to see Benny Goodman and the show, and the jitterbugs danced in the aisle and up on the stage. They had to call the police force to quiet them down… such a bunch of hoodlums! You never saw such.

    Well today F.D.R. and I celebrate another birthday… yessireee—yessireee—yessireee!

    It only means that I have known you one more year, one of the things I am grateful for.

    Thanks so much for that swell ending to your last letter. It was just like yourself, not mentioning the beginning of the letter.
"Luke"
My father's 28th birthday

Feb. 6, 1939

Dear Luther,

It was nice hearing from you and the news of the dance was colossal. We'll try not to have cause for delay this time so don't give it another thought.

I'm all aflutter, our neighbor Howard Button was wedded today to Hattie Tate. Weddings always excite me even when I can't witness them. Also Bob Highsmith and Ernestine Thomas are "dittoring" on Sunday. So you see we are all really beginning to live again, I mean some of us are.

Stork brought a son to the Harold Brown family and they are really very, very proud. And don't you dare call it a brat.

Can you imagine the S.S.Y. basketball team is playing in N.Y. on March 4th. They are praying for a safe return of all the members of the team after the heroic front they put on. It's really very sad and touching.

I must tell you of the shocks I had last night. I returned from work to find Bud and Bill Walker, Howard Brown, and a few other "small fry" sitting in our front room entertained by Lillian. It was really more than I could stand, so we oldsters went to the club in Scranton for recuperation.

Well that's all for this time, because after all I'm no Walter Winchell even if I do run a close second.

My sincerest congrats on your birthday. I know you'll have many more.

Mary

Hotel Wellington
Seventh Avenue
Fifty-Fifth and Fifty-Sixth Streets
New York

Feb. 11, 1939
N.Y.C.
Dear Mary,

    I gladly received your letter and it was nice you received the news pleasantly. It isn't the dance that so enthralled me, it was the fact that perhaps I'll have the opportunity of seeing you once again, and also your sister.

    Gee, people become married in Wilkes-Barre, that's strange. So weddings excite you, well we all have our favorite excitement although yours is fascinating. Well, and the stork still visits your community also? Also well. Good luck to the little squealer. I am the official uncle to three youngsters myself (I'm patting myself on the back.)

    I hope the S.S.Y. basketball team aren't venturing too far beyond their boundaries. I suppose it does grow tiresome and boring to play Scranton every week. I imagine the children have grown up quite a bit since I last saw them; don't be surprised at their tactics because they are trying to do what they see others do.

    Haven't been feeling so well last week. Nothing serious, just a cold and very stiff shoulder. If you were here you could rub my shoulder otherwise or I mean you not being here I had to do it myself. Feeling better but don't breathe a word about it because my mother would hear it and demand my home coming or something.

    So cheerio and waiting for an answer.
"Luke"
P.S. Thanks for the birthday congrats.

Feb. 17, 1939

Dear Luther,

It was as usual a delightful pleasure to hear from you. I was very sorry to read of your illness and doubly sorry that I could not be there to rub your shoulder. I am really very good at it. I had a slight touch of intestinal grippe myself. My dear mother put a mustard plaster on my stomach and I was burned redder than a raw steak. It was most uncomfortable and humiliating. I spent three days in bed. But I'm better too, thank you.

I've been working nights over at the hotel for Mr. Davis just until Lent. Mr. Cushioner is in a hotel in N.Y. now. He and I were good friends and I was sorry to hear of his leaving. Most of the employees have changed so you wouldn't be interested much any more.

Louise and her mother came home to live for a while, I mean they are in Scranton. Big stooge Louise coming back here—I was really surprised at her.

We are still looking forward to visiting you. I think Sara is bringing John Foster. They don't do anything or go anywhere without each other, poor things they've got it bad.

Well, please take good care of your cold because I'll tell your mother if you don't although I've refrained so far.

Mary

The Letters

Hotel Wellington
Seventh Avenue
Fifty-Fifth and Fifty-Sixth Streets
New York

Feb 25, 1939
N.Y.C.
Dear Mary:

Nice to hear that you received my letter so pleasingly, therefore I'm sending another. I'm fit as a fiddle now and ready for—oh you know. My stiffness and cold have vanished somewhat. You seem to have had an illness yourself. Well, be careful, Dear, we both cannot weaken. I know your little tender stomach was irritated from the nasty old plaster.

So you're in the hotel racket also—beware young lady, it is a bad business. Mr. Cushioner sought and found me and we had a bit of a chatter. It was rather amusing to hear of the Redington and its employees. They say all good friends must part. I hope you replace [him with] another.

Don't' be surprised to see anyone return to W-B. Time will bring each and every one back. It still was her home, as well as my home*. Someday I'll be back.

I received my invitation today. Please tell me if you received yours because I don't see John [Winfield] any more. But you know as far as you're concerned, you are taken care of but of course you wouldn't come alone. It's different now than it was last year—I don't stay at the house therefore, I didn't give him a list unless he has the one from last year. So you have less than two weeks. Hope to see you and write soon.
"Luke"

My father was responding to the mention of Louise Downey in my mother's previous letter.

Mar. 2, 1939
Dear Luther,

Yours was received with the usual pleasure. I was really glad to hear that your cold was so much better and that you were feeling so fit for everything.

By the way I want to thank you for the lovely, lovely valentine. It was really very sweet and I loved it.

Well, the team is ready to wipe up the city Saturday. I suppose some of them will be looking you up. If they need cheering I know you'll do your best like a nice boy.

Sara, John, Buddy and Margaret Foster are all very disappointed because we did not get invitations for the dance. So they asked me to write and tell you although I told them you didn't have anything to do with that. So if you get a few angry letters you'll know what it is all about. But they're coming to N.Y. whether they have a dance to go to or not.

I almost spoiled everything by falling down the stairs at work with a glass vase in my hand. I came out alright, though with a few minor cuts and the afternoon off. Not so bad, I might try it again sometime—from the bottom step!

[words crossed-out] That was some French but skip it.

Mary

Missing Letter

The Letters

Hotel Redington
Absolutely Fire Proof
Wilkes-Barre, Pa.

March 8, 1938*

Dear Luther,

Recognize the stationary? Mine ran out and Brother came to the rescue.

Well we are all ready for anything N.Y. has to offer. Sara and I have talked and talked until our family is nearly wacky. When one of us just says "new" they all run. Truth is they are all jealous, but they'll have their day.

We have been staying in all week to keep fit. Sara says if I get sleepy it'll be my funeral so I'm going to be very careful.

Our bus is leaving here at 1:30 Friday afternoon so we'll be in New York shortly after six o'clock. We're taking the Greyhound and praying there are no storms of any kind. Buses make me "jittery" and Sara won't ride a train. She thinks they're much too wobbly so I guess I'll make my debut by rail some other time.

See you soon,

Mary

My mother incorrectly dated the letter.

HOTEL REDINGTON
ABSOLUTELY FIREPROOF
WILKES-BARRE, PA.

March 8, 1938

Dear Luther

Recognize the stationary! Mine ran out and Brother came to the rescue.

Well we are all ready for any thing N.Y. has to offer. Sara and I have talked and talked until our family is nearly wacky. When of us just says "New" they all run. Truth is they are all jealous, but they'll have their day

The Letters

March 14, 1939

Dear Luther,

Now that I've spent a whole day resting I can write and thank you once more for the lovely time. It was terribly nice being with you and even the weather nor John, nor anything could spoil it. I say John because he is the worst thing I can imagine. He makes me angry just to look at him.

We arrived home safe and sound but dead tired at six o'clock Monday morning. It took us four hours just to come from Scranton. The bus ran out of gas in Pittston and we had to wait while they refueled. I think someone must have "jinxed" us. It couldn't have been just fate. My mother was waiting for us and I guess she nearly had a nervous breakdown. You know how mothers are with their horrible imaginations, et cetera.

I have been trying to learn to boogey. Sister is teaching us. So at least I'll feel like a colored girl. She says for anyone who can't "boogey" there is no sense in being colored. She was disgusted because Sara and I don't know how. Especially when we told her even the babies were trying to do it.

Well, thanks again Luther and please write soon. I feel sort of blue and I'm having a hard time writing this letter. My brain won't think for me.

Mary

Missing Letter

The Letters

From this letter I infer that my father was laid off from his job at the Hotel Wellington.

March ~~14~~ 21, 1939*
Dear Luther,

See when I wrote I couldn't even keep the date straight. I was a week behind the time. I'm slower than I thought.

I can hardly believe it's been only two weeks since we've been to N.Y. To me it seems like months.

I received your paper this morning and we were proud to see our names with such notables. Thank you so much for remembering to send it.

It is terribly sweet of you to want to tell me your troubles, Luther. I do want to hear everything concerning yourself you care to tell me. And do hope you have the very best of luck when the Fair opens. Soon you'll have so much to do you'll wish for a few leisure hours. That's the way it usually happens.

Well, Luther, we know now what everyone in Wilkes-Barre thinks of us. People I didn't know existed have told us or our friends how worried they were about our return from N.Y. I thought we planned our trip rather quietly but it seems that it was the talk of the town. I think if we went to Chicago they would have the band out to greet us on our return. But it was nice to know they care. A small town has its compensations at times. It makes us little "shots" feel big. Ask Greeney, he'll tell you.

Please give my regards to everyone.
Mary

*The correction is shown as it appears in Mary's letter.

Missing Letter

The Letters

March 28, 1939

Dear Luther,

Your girlfriend has been ill the last few days with a nasty cold. I frightened the family on Sunday with something resembling mumps but they disappeared yesterday, thank heavens.

I really enjoyed your <u>little</u> verse, please write some more.

I was sorry to read that our visit left you feeling lonely. But it [is] awfully sweet to know you care. Maybe it will help to know that I think of you at least a thousand times a day, maybe even more than that. I have a one track mind, so they tell me, I hadn't noticed myself.

My mother is baking cookies and I have to stop every few moments and do a bit of sampling. This happens to be one of my best accomplishments. I love the cookie dough as much as the finished product; hence, I'm very busy at such times. This is a secret I don't tell everyone, a hangover from my childhood.

I do hope you won't need an Egyptian consul to decipher this scratching. Sara thinks you will. She insists I invest in a typewriter and give my friends a break. I tell her to "hold tight," practice makes perfect. I'll be a handwriting genius, don't you hope?

Mary

Hotel Wellington
Seventh Avenue
Fifty-Fifth and Fifty-Sixth Streets
New York

April 1, 1939

Dear Mary:

Your sweet letter was received but your illness did not please me—hope you feel better when this letter reaches you.

Well everyone seems to be getting ready for Easter but it will be just another Sunday for me. We are putting on our new uniforms on Easter so it will be my new Easter outfit, thanks for that. I'm sure you are going to look very sweet. I wish I were there to see you. The avenue will be jumpin' down here. I'll be standing on the corner on 135th Street in case you pass by.

It's just wonderful to hear that you think of me so often, we seem to resemble each other in that matter. Please continue to do so and maybe we will be rewarded by seeing each other.

I thought Sis was the baby of the family and you were the eldest. I hope I haven't made an error. But I suppose nobody was home but you at the time so you couldn't resist the temptation of sampling your mother's cookie dough. Well, I'll be frank with you Mary, I use to do the same thing and wouldn't mind doing it again. Down here there are too many ahead of me. By the time I get the pan I can just hang it in the closet because it is a clean as though it were just bought. Woe is me!

I roomed Martha Tilton Thursday afternoon. She is Benny Goodman's vocalist. She only had twelve pieces of luggage and she isn't any larger than you. She was ill with a cold and so was the whole band, she said. They will be here in the hotel a week. As soon as the jitterbugs find out they will be ganging the place for autographs.

Well, my dear, since you enjoyed my little verse so much, I will write another. Maybe I was supposed to be a poet—maybe…

Well hold tight because it's coming

Swirling with glee,
When humor is portrayed,
You will plainly see,
Her glamour displayed.

"Luke"

Wilkes-Barre, Pa
April 6, 1939
Dear Luther,

Are you calling yourself Longfellow Snyder? As a poet you are simply colossal. Why don't you try a few smart, stream-lined verses for the World's Fair? I'm sure they would appreciate it if you would, and I'd be proud to say I knew you when.......

My cold is much better now, thank you. You know you can't keep a Brooks down long.

It was a pleasure to hear you say you would have a new uniform at least. I have to work on Sunday but I don't even get a new uniform. I'll stand in the lobby and discuss Easter outfits with the head usher. That will be all of the Easter parade I'll see. Lucky for me that he is a congenial chap. It's more fun when you can talk things over.

I think Sara is going to Port Chester, N.Y., with the Johnson family (again). I hope she has better luck this time.

Last Sunday we were surprised with a visit from Chris Hillman. He wanted to know about our trip to the big city. You know how we can rave.

Well, here are my very best wishes for a very Happy Easter and I do mean it.
Mary

Hotel Wellington
Seventh Avenue
Fifty-Fifth and Fifty-Sixth Streets
New York

April 10, 1939
N.Y.C.
Dear Mary,

I appreciated your letter very much. Nice to hear that you are recovering from your cold.

I hope you and the family enjoyed Easter…it was a very nice day. Alec Johnson from Reading came to Emily's while I was up there with two girls and a fellow so I went downtown with them. They wanted to go all over New York during their short stay, which could not be done. Alec told me about his affair with your friend Louise. He doesn't blame her, he blames it on his sudden misfortune. Perhaps it all happened for the best.

I hope Sara makes that delayed trip safely.

Chris was supposed to have let Charley and I know when he was coming to Wilkes-Barre. We would have come with him [even] if it were only for one day. That is all the time Charley could get off anyway but he didn't let us know.

I do not care to write any poetry for the World's Fair—it is for you exclusively. I have some more for you too. If you will accept them I'll write them.

Mrs. Boone and Jocelyn asked about you. I was down there Saturday night. The baby is walking now. She is real cute.

More next time….

The Verse

> She is easy to remember,
> And so hard to forget.
> In hot July and cold December,
> Always she is my pet.

Luke

P.S. I went to church Easter morning. How am I doin'?

Wilkes-Barre, PA
April 14, 1939
Dear Luther,

As usual it was a pleasure to hear from you. Your little verses improve with each letter you write and I do enjoy them very much. Please keep them up. You are very nice to make them exclusively mine and I appreciate that very much.

I just blew the top, Luther, when I read of your having been to church Easter Sunday morning. I know you were uplifted by the good will that prevailed there after. Going to church always gives you that special sort of feeling and I am always glad when I attended.

My sister and brother were there and I asked them to say a prayer for me. If I don't go soon I'm afraid something dreadful will happen. It's a sin to stay away so long. Well I feel better after that long confession. I don't mention very often of my long absence from church.

I was surprised to read of Alec Johnson's having visited with you. I had forgotten he existed to tell the truth. Louise has a new boyfriend now and he is really very nice. Maybe she'll have better luck this time. I hope.

If I had known Chris was here—that he had promised to bring you with him and didn't—I would have set him out on the sidewalk. The nasty thing, he never mentioned it, though he did say he saw you often. Maybe next time he will remember, at least I hope.

Please don't forget the verses and write soon.
Mary

Missing Letter

Hotel Redington
Absolutely Fireproof
Wilkes-Barre, PA

Wilkes-Barre, PA
April 20, 1939
Dear Luther,

    It was nice to receive your sweet "good morning" although it was just about twenty-four hours later. I think it must have been about 9:10 a.m. when I read your letter. Only I had been up for almost an hour. I usually arise about 8:20 and by 9:15 I am on my way to Kempton's Salon*. Doesn't that look "spiffy". I think I'll suggest it to the firm and maybe they'll promote me. They could use a brilliant young lady, I'm telling you!

    I was too surprised to read of Vernice's matrimonial venture. Too bad that there had to be a few "<u>buts</u>", whatever they were.

    Please tell Jocelyn that we haven't forgotten her and that she might write to us sometime. Also give our regards to Hayward.

    Howard Reid was home last week. The gang went out Sunday taking snapshots etc. Mary Buster was here also for "old home week." But I had to work so I missed the fun. Poor Mary, Griff and Georgia are, or rather, have been sent back to Kentucky. She and the "man without a country" may have something in common. She ought to have plenty to tell her grandchildren about her travels. I'll have to tell her to let me in on some of them. Can't let my grandchildren down.

    And, Luther, please don't leave all the confessing for me to do. You know how very modest I am.

Don't forget the poetry—I love it.
Mary

*The name of the store where my mother worked was Kempton's. She was quite pleased with herself for adding "salon" to the name.

Missing Letter

The Letters

Wilkes-Barre, PA
April 26, 1939
Dear Luther,

    I will just have to write N.Y mail authorities and see why they are so slow. When I write to you I expect everyone concerned between here and N.Y. to cooperate in seeing that you get the most prompt delivery. The nerve of them keeping you waiting until ten o'clock!

    Please tell Mrs. Lawrence I appreciate her interest and she should just keep up the good work. I do hope, though, that she doesn't have to do much checking up on you.

    Thank you so much for those very encouraging words, they are just what I needed. I have a bad case of spring fever right now, maybe, that is why I resent working every day. That old saying "all work and no play makes Jack a dull boy" implies for Jill, too, and I don't want to be a totem pole all my life. Someday I'll just "blow the top" and scandalize this whole town, at least that's the way I feel tonight.

    As for Howard's talking so much, I don't know. You see, I didn't see him, not being here when he called, but I suppose he does.

    Your confessions are still very nice and I appreciate them more than ever.

Answer soon.
Mary

Hotel Wellington
Seventh Avenue
Fifty-Fifth and Fifty-Sixth Streets

New York
April 28, 1939
N.Y.C

Dear Mary:

So glad to receive your letter. The service was more prompt this time. I think it has been recognized that we weren't pleased.

Howard, Wilmer, and Edgar were down here. We went out with John Winfield Wednesday night stagging and had loads of fun. We went to the Elks Rendezvous, I suppose you remember that place, and also to the Mineo.

They only stayed for the one day so their time was very limited. They promised faithfully that they would return this summer. I hope they do and also you of course. We visited Maude and Milton. That was a request of Edgar's. Milt is a jitterbug hundred percent. He's a crazy cat! He also asked about you and Sara.

The fair opens Sunday, so we can look forward to seeing eight million more plus the millions that are here. If I ever come to W-B you'll have to keep crowds of people in the streets or I'll probably go mad.

Well you said you liked it so here is more:

> So neat in her togs,
> Regardless of the dress.
> In sunshine, storms or fogs
> Vogue she does encompass.

"Luke"

The Letters

Wilkes-Barre, PA
May 1, 1939
Dear Luther,

I suppose you are very busy now with the rush of the big fair. I listened to the broadcast yesterday afternoon. It sounded very pompous and ceremonial but I enjoyed it.

Was it raining in NY, it rained here, but I guess people didn't mind that—not much.

Harold has been here telling of his visit with you. He seems to have enjoyed the trip very much. You must tell your friend John that he is a very lucky man. The boys have done nothing but rave over his very charming wife. They admire her very much and you know of course, that we do.

We also heard of Maud's big stepson. She must have her hands full with so many men to take care of. She certainly has my sympathy.

By the way, tell Hayward that I heard Bing Crosby sing in his latest picture and for the first time I really enjoyed his singing. You remember we couldn't agree on that score.

I am all a "dither." We have been invited to three formals. Bethlehem, Binghamton and Scranton. We are going to Bethlehem on Friday night. I'll think of you every dance and wish you were there.

If you happen to hear the song, "If I Didn't Care" think of me. It leaves me weak in the knees.
Mary

Dear Mary, Dear Luther

Hotel Wellington
Seventh Avenue
Fifty-Fifth and Fifty-Sixth Streets
New York

May 5, 1939
N.Y.C

Dear Mary:

We are busy as you surmised, people coming from and going to the fair. This hotel and many others are like mad-houses. All I hear from morning to night is fair-fair-fair! Both at work and from work but I might as well get used to it because that is what I'm going to contend with for the rest of the summer at least.

Today (Fri.) is my day off and what a relief. It's nice to be working but so pleasant to have a day off. I'll donate this entire day to special thoughts of you.

Sunday until about 6 p.m. here was very nice but after that it clouded up and we had showers. Everyone seems to admire Jocelyn. I hope John does. She feels the same way about you all or all of you.

Hayward was very pleased that you recognize his favorite vocalist. If Bing was a lady it's no telling what Hayward would to do hear her sing. He was a man all for the best I'm afraid.

It's swell to hear you've gotten so many bids for those June dances. All of them are very well conducted and I'm sure you'll enjoy yourself at any of them. Here is hoping that you and your party enjoy yourselves to the utmost at the Bethlehem affair. Thanks so much for wishing for me. I've done the same for you often.

We are on daylight saving time, you know, and it makes the day longer. Has your city adopted it also?

It's strange but the same number, "If I didn't Care" sort of makes me woozy too.

The Letters

Your verse:
>   A coiffure well arranged,
>   To equal her grace
>   With hair unashamed
>   To make her winning face.

"Luke"

Answer soon

I heard many times about my mother's plane ride. As the story was told, she rode in an open-air, two-seater propeller plane. She was so frightened she tried to climb out of the plane mid-air. She didn't fly again until she was fifty-five.

Wilkes-Barre, Pa
May 10, 1939
Dear Luther,

So nice to hear from you. Please don't work so hard over those Fair viewers. They will be coming for the next couple of years so you may just as well take your time. After all they aren't real New Yorkers and won't expect to be rushed any way. They probably want to take things a little slower.

Thank you kindly for those special thoughts. If there were such a thing as mental telepathy those thoughts would have been great consolation. It was my misfortune to have to work Friday night and I missed the dance. I sat in the check room at the club and wished I were anywhere in the world but W-B. China even looked good to me. But I'll just cross my fingers and wish for better luck for the next affair.

I have been awarded Sundays as my day off. I felt like a lamb at a spring frolic. The kids treated me like a long lost friend. I almost forgot to tell you about my aeroplane ride Sunday afternoon. The nicest part was getting my feet back on the ground. The pilot did some fancy flying and I almost died. I'm afraid planes are just a little too modern for me.

Well, toodle-loo and don't wait long to answer.
Mary

According to the web page 'Primarily A Capella Singers.com', the Ink Spots, a doo-wop quartet, scored a huge hit with "If I Didn't Care." The web page reports that it sold 19 million copies worldwide.

Hotel Wellington
Seventh Avenue
Fifty-Fifth and Fifty-Sixth Streets
New York

May 15, 1939
N.Y.C
Dear Mary:

Received your interesting missive. We aren't rushing any more than necessary so you need not worry.

Your friends Jean and Rudy walked in on me last Monday night. They caught me in the bath tub around 9 p.m. and was getting ready for bed. They just couldn't believe I was going to bed that early. So I dressed and took them out although they had to make their bus at 12:15 so you see there was not much time to go any place. I had to get up early the next morning also. They wanted to go to the Savoy so that is where we went for the ensuing two or three hours. We had to leave during the most interesting part of the time we were there and that was the broadcast. I asked them why they didn't bring you all with them. They at least could ask you if you wanted to go anyway, that goes for anyone else who comes down from up there.

Emily called me up and told me her mother was down so I went up and had the favorite home town chat with her.

I must tell you about the swell show I saw at the Apollo. The Ink Spots were in and they sang "If I Didn't Care" just like you hear it on the recording. The house went mad. Then the vocalist with Claude

Hopkins orchestra sang another number that sends you, "Don't You Worry About Me." The whole show was exceptionally good.

It seems as though if anyone is left behind it's you what causes that. Well, you can always wish for another dance—better luck next time.

It's quite a feat having an aeroplane ride, that is something I have never had. Probably you will be inspired to become a queen of the air.

Well keep sweet and answer soon

> Where ever she may be,
> China, Norway or home,
> She is very dear to me,
> Although I love to roam.

Luke

May 19, 1939
Wilkes-Barre, Penna.
Dear Luther,

It was so very nice of you to want Rudy to bring us down to N.Y. with him. He had told us of his visit with you and of how much he enjoyed his brief stay.

So you're trying my methods of early to bed and early to rise. I didn't think you would even succumb to such early hours. I have been retiring earlier and earlier. I think it was Tuesday I was in bed by six-thirty. I felt like I had been high for a week on Wednesday.

I must not forget to tell you about the nice affair we attended in Binghamton this week. Claude Hopkins' orchestra played. Orlando Robeson and Beverly White were the vocalists. They played my favorite "If I Didn't Care" several times. I think it must have been the favorite of a good many people.

I suppose between Mrs. Haley and you, we Wilkes-Barreans were put on the spot but we care not what you say as long as it's nice.

Luther, my mother asked me to thank you for the beautiful card on Mother's Day. She was really touched to think that you remembered her.

Your verses are improving and each one has been most appreciated.
Mary
P.S. My brother just took me for a ride in bedroom slippers and my hair braided on each side. Me!

Hotel Wellington
Seventh Avenue
Fifty-Fifth and Fifty-Sixth Streets
New York

May 26, 1939
N.Y.C.

Dear Mary:

Enjoyed your letter very much. I like very much going to bed early and rising early as you do. The most pleasant time of the day is between six and twelve noon.

Everything is beginning to look very pleasing. The parks are beginning to get a break. They have put water in the pool and people are talking of going to the beaches. I like that.

So glad to hear you enjoyed yourself at the dance in Binghamton. Your enjoyment is my pleasure.

Mrs. Haley is riding you Wilkes-Barreans but she doesn't mean it. I still think all of you are swell although I have been away from you for a little while.

Glad your mother received and liked the little card. Mothers are fascinating people any way—they are great people too!

Perhaps your brother will be down some time with the family. Maybe. It's nice he's driving now. It will be your turn soon to learn to drive. Wouldn't you like to learn? Mrs. Lawrence is taking driving lessons now. She is doing very well.

Well more next time and answer soon.

> This poem is humble,
> But rich in its air.
> Could I write and jumble,
> If I didn't care?

"Luke"

The Letters

June 2, 1939

Dear Luther,

Does your head go round and round while your heart stands still? Mine does. But that doesn't mean I'm dizzy.

Did you have an enjoyable holiday? I hope you did, 'cause then mine will have been that much more enjoyable.

I know that you are in your glory now that the beaches and parks are open. Have you been swimming yet? I have had the opportunity but not the time. I hope to go soon though.

I'll have to tell you that I have little desire to learn to drive but I wait patiently for Sara to learn. You know Sara is as indispensable as my right arm. I don't know what I'd do without her.

By the way, have you seen John? He has been in N.Y. I think he intends to stay awhile. Also Art Sands. He intends to look you up to surprise you. Isn't that nice? You see you still retain your popularity in your old home town!

Please don't wait too long to answer.

Mary

The Park Central
Seventh Avenue
55th to 56th Street
New York NY

June 9, 1939

Dear Mary:

Unaccustomed as I am of writing letters to you, I really think I'll find it a thrill to correspond with you, what do you think?

Thanks, because the feeling about the holiday is mutual. We're having another holiday here on Saturday. Their Highnesses, the King and Queen of England will be here. I suppose while you're reading this scribbling, crowds will be cheering them or perhaps jeering them. Perhaps, Kingie and Queenie and myself will get together and see if we can arrange for me to be King for a while. Well so much for the new King.

Hayward, Jocelyn, John and myself with a few others had a swell time the other night at a dance. It was an organdy dance. All the females wore organdy dresses. It was trés chic, as we French would say.

I heard John was in town but we just couldn't seem to get together. Tell him I'm sorry I missed him every time he called. Haven't seen Art yet. You'll notice I am using some of my neighbor's stationary for a change.

Well I suppose that is all the dirt for this time.

Enhance her with flowers
Forever and a day
In our private bower
If I had my way

"Luke"

P.S. Gee…I almost forgot to tell you about Mrs. Lawrence's dream. She dreamt that Sarah was visiting her and when she was leaving, Sarah gave her a five and ten dollar bill…of course every time Mrs. Lawrence has a dream, money must be involved. But tell Sarah if this comes true, please bring you with her. Thank you.

Wilkes-Barre, Pa
June 16, 1939
Dear Luther,

It was, as always, a pleasure to hear from you. I hope you become accustomed soon, to corresponding with me. It really shouldn't be a hard job when I'm such a simple-minded person.

Well I suppose you had the pleasure of meeting the King and Queen. A person of your importance and popularity could not have missed such an occasion. If you have, Sara wants you to please send her your autograph for her scrap book. She also was thrilled with the dream Mrs. Lawrence had. She is terribly put out that dreams don't come true, at least once in a while. She'd love to be known as philanthropist, she is such a generous soul.

This has been an uneventful week. Huber Stephenson and Pauline Johnson announced their coming marriage which is sometime this month. Chuck Fisher and Naomi Tate are being wed to-morrow. Cupid has been doing double duty here. He missed our family as usual.

My sister graduated yesterday. I helped her celebrate last night chaperoning her crowd.

Please excuse this terrible penmanship. I'll surprise you next time.
Mary

The Letters

Hotel Wellington
Seventh Avenue
Fifty-Fifth and Fifty-Sixth Streets
New York

[undated]

Dear Mary:

Received your very newsy letter, thank you. Up there, they are becoming hitched while down here they are trying very hard to become unhitched. I was a witness for one couple getting a divorce last week. We had to go through the court order just like you read in the paper everyday only ours was in a smaller scale.

It was quite amusing listening to the other cases before ours. In case you don't know, in New York state there is but one way to receive a divorce and that is through adultery. You can imagine some of the tales I heard. Ours was all fine and agreeable between both him and her so it was granted without trouble.

Gee, please congratulate your sister Lillian for me. Doesn't that make you feel older? Me too! I can't imagine you being chaperone though because that is the part for an old lady.

I met Chris Hillman at the La Ma Cherie Sunday night—loads of fun. He is coming home soon he said, I think I'll be home for a few days in September—not before that I guess.

Will you all be down here before then, do you think? You will I'm sure.

Jocelyn and Mrs. Boone asked about you again, in fact they continue to ask.

Well I think that is the business for this session. Perhaps I'll have more next time. So try and keep cool until then. This is a reminder:

Dear Mary, Dear Luther

> A little sip of wine
> Or a big scent of rye
> In this beverage line,
> She is a very small fry.

"Luke"

The Letters

Blanche Calloway was the older sister of Cab Calloway. According to the 'African American Registry.com', she enjoyed a music career that spanned over fifty years. She was one of the few women to ever to lead an all-male orchestra, 'Blanche Calloway and her Joy Boys'.

June 29, 1929
Dear Luther,

As usual, it was a royal treat to hear from you.

Chris was here over the week-end. Both he and George were in Scranton Sunday night and they dropped by the Tyler's where we had been invited to dinner. He mentioned his having seen you, also that you've been holding out on me. Is that the proper way to treat a friend?

We attended a nice dance in Scranton Monday night. Blanche Calloway played. I was sort of disappointed in the band. I guess I expected too much.

I was surprised when I saw that Mrs. Haley had arrived home on Sunday. She has been telling us of her visit all week. We were really excited, just hearing about it. I suppose, now, your mother will be next. She is very enthusiastic to say the least.

Andy MacDonald has been here for the last two or three weeks. We have loads of fun with him. By the way we have sort of gathered a pretty nice crowd now. It is comprised of married and single couples. We do have some gala times, I must admit. Every time we meet there are never less than ten or fifteen of us and a couple of times we had twenty in our crowd. So if you happen to come home in September, and I hope you do, it won't be quite so dead.

It would be much nicer if you could come sooner. You know anytime would be fine.

More next time.
Mary

Hotel Wellington
Seventh Avenue
Fifty-Fifth and Fifty-Sixth Streets
New York

July 4, 1939

Dear Mary:

Thanks a million for your letter…it would seem very lonesome if I didn't read one of your letters now and then.

I suppose this isn't news but Lois, Edna, Alice and Sara [Moss] were in town last week. I came home one day and found a note telling me they had called and the address to find them. We had quite a week-end.

I don't know what Chris told you about me but I cannot see where the holding out part fits in. Wait 'til I see him.

You and I have the same conception of Blanch Calloway, I think she smells on ice—meaning her band is terrible.

When you receive this letter you will have seen Mrs. Bush, Emily and Sonny. I guess I'm a telling ya any who!

Gee, you have quite a gang in the old Burg, nice going pal. I shall look forward to coming home in September. If I can see myself getting away before, perhaps I will.

I hope you enjoyed the 4th of July with much fun and hilarity. I'm spending a quiet one myself but don't mind.

Since first we met
Interest grew strong.
And I dare not let
Myself be wrong.

"Luke"

Answer soon

The Letters

July 9, 1939

Wilkes-Barre, Penna.

Dear Luther,

It was so very nice to hear from you. I appreciate your letters very much.

I saw and met all of your cousins and their families. They have quite a gang I must say.*

Like you I spent a quiet 4th. We attended a small picnic out in the country. I prefer parks.

Well there was another wedding today. Certainly are having an epidemic of marriages. The love bug just killing himself in this vicinity.

Grace Fisher is being wed soon also. Well more power to them.

I heard about Edna, and her troupe visiting the "big city." It was so nice of you to show them a good time.

Did you know Sara has a new baby? I mean of course Sara Moss, not my sister. I don't see how she could have gone to New York so soon. Well I guess everything becomes easier with practice.

Please try hard to visit us real soon and stop kidding me.

Mary

P.S.

Your verses couldn't be sweeter and I do appreciate them.

Luther's seven uncles and most of his first cousins were childless, so I believe the cousins were the Fishers. Luther's second cousin Elmer had seven children.

Hotel Wellington
Seventh Avenue
Fifty-Fifth and Fifty-Sixth Streets
New York

July 15, 1939

Dear Mary:

I was told by Emily that she saw you and the family. It was quite interesting to hear her telling about their reunion. I haven't met some of them myself. They perhaps will get together on another holiday and I'll make my earnest effort to be there.

Sister Mary is there any single people in W-B besides you and Sara? If there are I think I'll come back as a preacher…probably I can pick up a marriage or so now and then. Well alright!

I hear the picnic is on the 27th I'm sure you will attend it. I guess I'll have to miss it again to my regret—there ain't no justice. The thing I really was hoping, was a visit from your or my mother so I could take you to the fair. I haven't attended it yet thinking that you would come down. You know I just love being with you.

The Lawrences have checked out and gone to the country for the summer. I sleep downstairs now. I have lots of room if you could come.

I'm so glad that you like my simple verses. I didn't intend to continue as far as I did but you said you liked them. I'm just about running out but I'm still trying.

> Deep through the night
> And during the sultry day
> Would be a delight
> To be near her and not away.

"Luke"

<u>Please write soon.</u>

Hotel Redington
Absolutely Fireproof
Wilkes-Barre, Pa.

July 21, 1939

Dear Luther,

Your delightful little missive was much enjoyed.

I was much surprised the other day to receive a letter from Chris. George wrote Sara. They sort of had a homesick feeling I guess. Wonders never cease.

It was sweet of you to want to go to the fair with us. I want to visit you very much this summer and see New York during some fair weather. My vacation has been changed, I found out to my disappointment. It was supposed to have been the second and third week in August but now I am not sure when it will be. I think the last of August. Then try to keep me away.

The picnic next week is the least of my anticipations. I am going just for the dance at night and it had better be good.

Sonny has been having a wonderful time. I never knew there were so many kids in the neighborhood until he came along. A cute little girl came around last night and did they quarrel. Some technique.

Keep cool and answer soon.

Mary

Hotel Wellington
Seventh Avenue
Fifty-Fifth and Fifty-Sixth Streets
New York

July 28, 1939

Dear Mary:

I hope and trust that you enjoyed yourself at the picnic dance. I hope the weather was more favorable there than here.

Whenever you decide and can come down this summer you are graciously welcome. Jocelyn dreamt about Sarah last week. You see Mary, I monopolize all your dreams so that no one else can dream of you.

That Sonny seems to carry a certain technique for the fairer sex. I presume it must be his uncle Paul whom he takes after.

I attended a broadcast a couple of weeks ago and I am going again this Monday, July 31st. It is the Model Tobacco program 8:30 to 9 p.m. station WABC. Listen in and try to detect my laughs and applauds.

Take care of yourself and answer soon.

Her type is few
And without a doubt
Promenade a la rue
When you take her out

"Luke" (note the French)

The Letters

Wilkes-Barre, Pa
August 4, 1939
Dear Luther,

It was as usual so swell to hear from you.

So you're coming up in the world attending big broadcasts. Maybe someday someone will ask you to audition and you can recite your lovely verses to the accompaniment of some sweet organ music…Oh me!

We had rainy weather for the picnic, although it was cleared up for the evening. I'm sure everyone enjoyed themselves though.

Emily and Sonny are getting ready to come home now. Sonny has been very spoiled by his relatives, even his girlfriend has ceased to come around. He must resemble his uncle Paul in more ways than one.

Well, my vacation begins on the 13th of August. I don't know whether that's a good date or not. I'm trying not to be superstitious but I wish they'd give me Saturday off and sort of change the date. You can look for me any date after that. That is of course if your mother has completed her visit. I don't want to encroach on her time because I know she hasn't seen you in a long time and is looking eagerly toward visiting with you.

Thanks so much for saving a space for me in your dreams. You, of course, know what mine are.
Mary

Hotel Wellington
Seventh Avenue
Fifty-Fifth and Fifty-Sixth Streets
New York

Aug. 7, 1939
N.Y.C

Dear Mary:

Nice hearing from you again.

Your vacation is of great interest to me so I am answering immediately. You can come down on the 13th if you want to, don't hesitate because of Mother—we can make out alright. Besides she is coming home on the 14th. Olan is coming down on the 13th also. So why not contact him and that will be company for your trip. Is Sara coming too?

I saw Sonny this morning and my mother late last night and this morning. I guess she told me everything there is to know about W-B during that tenure so the rest of her stay here I can tell her about this city.

Sorry you had a bad picnic day but knowing you enjoyed yourself is a consolation.

So don't hesitate to come as soon as you can and write me details as soon as you find them out—if you come by bus or train on the 13th, please arrange to arrive after 3:30 p.m. day-light saving then I can meet you easily. Please don't hesitate to come and answer as soon as possible.

News of her coming
Is a great delight
Birds will be humming
During her flight

"Luke"

The Letters

The following events were reported extensively in 'The Morning Press', Bloomsburg's local paper. On the evening of August 7th, 1939, my mother's 40 year-old cousin Frank Parks Jr., met some friends for drinks. He arrived home where he lived with his parents, Frank Sr., and Hattie, in the early morning hours of August 8th. He disrobed in the living room where he slept on a cot, and then went upstairs to use the bathroom. His father, Frank Sr., was home alone and asked his son where Hattie had gone. Frank Jr. told him that she had gone to Catawissa because of the illness of one of their daughters. Frank Jr. then added, "You ought to know."

This remark enraged the elder Parks who had a vicious temper. He started to curse and struck Frank Jr. in the chest and pushed him, causing a kerosene lamp to be knocked over. Frank Jr. became enraged. He pushed back at his father and struck him several times with his fists. He then went downstairs but could hear his father continuing to curse him. He thought his father was coming downstairs to continue the quarrel and returned upstairs with a fireplace poker, intending to scare his father. His father grabbed him about the waist, and Frank Jr. struck back with the poker, bashing his father's skull.

When the police came, they found Frank Sr.'s body at the foot of the stairs. They concluded from the evidence that Frank Jr. had killed his father upstairs and tried to cover up his actions by pushing his father's body down the stairs. Frank initially denied any complicity in his father's death but confessed after sixteen hours of interrogation, pleading self-defense. He was charged with second degree murder and a trial date was set for October.

I don't know when my mother actually learned of this. Initially, her parents may have sheltered her from the news since there is no mention or hint of these events in my mother's letters to my father. I know it was a traumatic memory for her. Many times while I was growing up, she repeated the story of how "my cousin killed his father."

Wilkes-Barre, Pa
August 10, 1939
Dear Luther,

Thanks a million for those nice thoughts on my birthday. I had an enjoyable day just in case you're interested.

I know your mother and you have been doing the rounds of the big city and the fair. We Wilkes-Barreans certainly keep you busy.

Luther, since you say that you will not be inconvenienced by my arriving on Sunday I will be there on the 6:35 Greyhound. That is Standard time. 7:35 your time.

Sara's vacation is over so she will not be able to come with me much to her disappointment. We couldn't arrange them together as mine has been changed so often.

If there is any way that I am inconveniently in the way or upsetting any plans any one has made please don't hesitate to write and let me know. I can always come later.

Mary

Hotel Wellington
Seventh Avenue
Fifty-Fifth and Fifty-Sixth Streets
New York

Aug. 11, 1939
N.Y.C
Dear Mary:
    Will meet you at the same station you came in before at 7:30 PM.
    Glad you are coming
"Luke"
P.S.
The station is on 50th Street in case you have forgotten

Wilkes-Barre, PA
August 22, 1939
Dear Luther,

I know you are busy resting after <u>my</u> vacation. I don't think I'll ever be the same again.

I did have a fine time and I want you to know that I appreciate very much you letting me spend my vacation with you. It was the very nicest way I could have spent it.

We arrived home about four-thirty our time on Sunday afternoon. My folks were surprised to see me so early. It was almost two o'clock when we left N.Y. Blanch and Olin went shopping for World's Fair souvenirs and we waited for them on 42nd St. I didn't mind though, there was so much to look at that the time just flew.

I haven't seen your mother since I've been home. But Mother said that she was so tired when she came off the train she staggered. She waited until Thursday to come up and tell about her trip. She can talk about it as well as I can.

Well, Luther, since I haven't heard any news since I've been home, I can't write any to you. So I close and go to bed. It's about eight o'clock and that is my bed time from now until Christmas.

Answer soon

Mary

Give my regards to everyone and tell Jocelyn to please write me. Mary

The Letters

Hotel Wellington
Seventh Avenue
Fifty-Fifth and Fifty-Sixth Streets
New York

August 28, 1939
N.Y.C
Dear Mary:

So pleased of your safe arrival home. You made very good time.

Very much elated over the fact that you enjoyed your short vacation—it would have been short to me if you would have stayed a year. Your pleasure is my happiness.

Met Jocelyn on the avenue Sunday night—conveyed your message to her and she said she would write; although, she is busy trying to become a free woman again. That was all our chat was about.

Chris came to the house Sunday evening also. We rode around for a short while. He picked up George and they went to work.

So if I come home you are going to bed at 8:30 P.M. That's a fine howdy-do. But I bet you won't. Well I hope you have recuperated by the time this missive reaches you. I have rested up pretty will now and I plan to keep rested until I come home—I hope.

Well keep sweet and answer soon.
"Luke"

My mother alludes to the ominous news about Germany's invasion of Poland, and France and Great Britain's declaration of war against Germany.

Wilkes-Barre, Pa
September 5, 1939
Dear Luther,

Did you have a gay holiday week-end? We spent ours <u>very</u> quietly. Selina Edwards brought a couple of cousins home with her and we helped to entertain them. I never really saw a better example of a couple of "squares". But we had to live up to our name as the Wilkes-Barre hostesses.

I am fully recovered from my vacation now and ready for almost anything. So you needn't worry about when you come home; I'll be able to keep up with the best of you and your late hours.

The radio is on and I can hardly control my pen; it wants to do a "boogey" on me.

They are broadcasting a favorite of mine, the "Muskrat Rambler" an old song that is awful mellow, at least I think so. But then I like so many you can't ever keep up with me.

Believe it or not I have not been dancing for almost six weeks. Better be careful when you come home. I'll probably kill myself!

Are you all ready to shoulder your musket and don your uniform, because I'm afraid you'll need them soon. I think I'm going to practice up on my knitting because somebody might need a scarf. That's about as much as I'll get done.

Well that is all for this time.
Mary

Hotel Wellington
Seventh Avenue
Fifty-Fifth and Fifty-Sixth Streets
New York

Sept. 11, 1939
N.Y.C.
Dear Mary:

I spent a very quiet week-end also.

Since you say you are all rested and recovered from your vacation, perhaps I shall take mine—yep I shall. You have a date with me Thursday night about 9:30 p.m. Tell Sara not to be home.

I think I shall come home for the holiday. I suppose my Jewish friends will be home also.

Perhaps I'll bring the World's Fair with me—yep, I shall. Have the backyard ready.

I'd better see you folks before I am called to arms also.

I'll see you soon.

"Luke"

Hotel Wellington
Seventh Avenue
Fifty-Fifth and Fifty-Sixth Streets
New York

September 20, 1939
N.Y.C.

Dear Mary:

I have returned to repeat that hustle and bustle again. You don't realize how much I enjoyed those few days of relaxation.

Mary, you were swell and each moment I spend with you is a treasure itself. I hope it will not be as long before I see you again. You have gotten under my skin pretty well now and I like it. I really enjoyed seeing you. It makes me feel as though I have something to live for. I hope everything runs along smooth so that I can carry-out my intentions.

I haven't seen anyone but Mrs. Lawrence and Champ and they were very anxious to know how you were. I was pleased to tell them too. Write Jocelyn because should I see her, I am going to tell her [how] you are.

Stay as sweet as you are and please answer soon.

"Luke"

Wilkes-Barre, PA
September 25, 1939
Dear Luther,

    It was really a rare treat to have you in our city. I am so terribly sorry though that there wasn't more in the way of entertainment. Next time we'll try to plan more so you won't think we are always so lonesome.

    I hope you have relayed my very best regards to everyone, as I may have forgotten to mention it.

    Tell Jocelyn that I intend to write soon and I do expect her to answer, at least a post card to let me know she received my letter.

    My mother was so pleased to hear from you. She thinks you are really fine yourself and you are graciously welcome in our home at any time, please remember that.

    I guess that is all for this time. Please answer soon.

Mary

P.S. I dreamed a terrible dream of you the other night so be careful.

Nineteen thirty-nine was a huge year for the Glenn Miller Orchestra. The Orchestra's current web page lists several 1939 hits including 'Moonlight Serenade', 'Stairway to the Stars', and 'Over the Rainbow'.

Hotel Wellington
Seventh Avenue
Fifty-Fifth and Fifty-Sixth Streets
New York

September 30, 1939
N.Y.C.
Dear Mary:

So very glad to receive such a sweet letter. I really want to say that I enjoyed every minute I spent in <u>your</u> city. Just the privilege of seeing you every night was a pleasure in itself.

I hope I deserve all of your cordial welcomes—they are pleasing.

I must tell you about the show I saw. So very sorry you couldn't see it—honest. It was Glenn Miller and his orchestra plus the famous "If I Didn't Care" boys. The show really came on. They wouldn't let the Ink Spots off the stage.

I got a new radio today. It's jumping now with music by "The Count". Champ just left—he went with me to get it. It will help keep me in on these cold winter nights. I'm going to save myself for you.

Well your terrible dream hasn't taken action as yet but I hope it doesn't but I'll be careful. Especially for you.
"Luke"

The Letters

Wilkes-Barre, Pa
October 6, 1939
Dear Luther,

It was a pleasure to hear from you. I always look forward to receiving your letters. They are the sunshine of my life.

I was glad to read of your buying a radio for your room. I know you will derive a lot of pleasure from it. I am glad you enjoyed my orchestra and my "If I Didn't Care" boys. I haven't heard either of them for some time. But will catch up some day I hope.

I have a new favorite now, Johnny Davies. His rendition of "Pretending" just leaves me breathless.

Bill Grimes was here the other night. He says that card you dropped him was a "killer." It was nice of you to have remembered so well. He is coming to N.Y. soon; to get another hat I guess (he hasn't bought one in quite a while).

Give my regards to everyone and answer real soon.
Mary

On October 9th, the day before this letter was written, Frank Parks Jr. was sentenced to a maximum of ten to twenty years for the second degree murder of his father. His mother and two of his sisters had testified at the sentencing hearing that Frank Sr. had been a vicious man and that Frank Jr. had been a man of mild temperament. Hattie told the court he was a "good boy" who had come home to live when all his siblings had moved away. The 'Bloomsburg Morning Press' news article stated that as the sentence was pronounced, Frank appeared stunned and Hattie cried softly.

Hotel Wellington
Seventh Avenue
Fifty-Fifth and Fifty-Sixth Streets
New York

October 10, 1939
N.Y.C.

Dear Mary:

So much pleasure is absorbed by your letters. Please continue to send them.

Sonny asked me about you the other day. He can remember the better things in life already.

I really do appreciate my little radio. I heard a very pretty number the other night, please listen for it if you haven't already heard of it. The name of it is "My Prayer." By the way your favorite is breath-taking. We both do appreciate music. I'm so glad.

Everyone glad to hear from you. Keep well and sweet.

"Luke"

Sunday
October 15, 1939
Dear Luther,

It was just swell hearing from you. The pleasure is really all mine.

I was a good girl and went to church this morning. I think this is the second time I've attended since you were here. So you see I am improving.

The Wrights were here during the week. Challsy and Ozzie are being married soon so they were paying their respects to we poor things who didn't have a chance. You're slipping, you failed to relay to me the fact that Bernice had a son. The boys were shocked when they learned of our not knowing.

Your mother was here the other night on her way to "Bingo." You still have second place in her affections.

Can you imagine after losing that hideous wart on my forehead, I have the most awful looking boil on my arm. I'm positively disgusted. I must have done something terribly bad to deserve this. Maybe your girlfriend isn't so nice after all. I'm a mystery to myself, doing things behind my back.

Be good and write soon.
Mary
P.S. Your song was lovely. It's one of my special favorites.

My father had a knack for telling funny stories and jokes. When he was "on," he would be the star of the party.

Hotel Wellington
Seventh Avenue
Fifty-Fifth and Fifty-Sixth Streets
New York

October 23, 1939
N.Y.C.

Dear Mary:

Your soothing letter was graciously received and enjoyed very much. Nice to hear of your religious progress—swell.

I wonder if you heard me laughing between eight and nine o'clock Sunday night—you should have because I was listening to Charlie McCarthy. He had me in stitches.

I was to dinner Sunday evening to Champ's residence. This was the second Sunday dinner I have eaten since I returned from Wilkes-Barre. You know how I star in those Sunday evening dinners.

Are the Wrights going to incorporate?

Think nothing of those warts and boils, they come and go like the wind.

I have another song. The name of it is "So Many Times." The last words of the song are, "To hear you confess and care, has been my prayer, so many times." If I seem a bit sentimental at times, don't blame me, blame yourself.

You have been asked about by Marie, Champ and Mrs. Lambert although she does not know you yet.

Please be careful.

"Luke"

The Letters

Ventriloquist Edgar Bergen based his 'dummy' Charlie McCarthy on an Irish newsboy he knew. The web page, 'Charlie McCarthy.org' describes Charlie as a wisecracking teenager who radio censors allowed to get away with double entendre and sexual innuendo that the same censors rejected for live performers.

Wilkes-Barre
October 30, 1939
Dear Luther,

It was so nice to hear from you again, your little missives are really a great source of pleasure. It was nice reading of your having been invited out to dinner. I happened to be dining out myself the same Sunday. So you really weren't the only one playing your star roll.

Does Charlie McCarthy affect you in the same way? His program left me with a bad case of hiccups. He's really a killer.

We had a big surprise last week. Wash Downey was in town. He came around a couple of times but I didn't happen to be at home. I was sorry though, to have missed him.

Incidentally, Mary Buster spent several days with us last week. That girl is a mess; she's crazier than a loon, I swear.

We went to a party last night. For a change it was a "hard" affair*. It was after four this morning when we got in and I feel beat to my socks. I never worked a longer day in my life and kept a permanent yawn on my face all day. It's about 7:45 so in about ten more minutes I'll be in bed. You'll probably hear me sigh all the way in N.Y.

Your song is a fine number, but "My Prayer" still rates top with me.
Mary
*Liquor was served.

Hotel Wellington
Fifty-Fifth and Fifty-Sixth Streets
New York

November 5, 1939

N, Y.C.

Dear Mary:

Thanks a million for your letter—I enjoyed it. Some of those fine dances will be in operation soon. The first one I will attend will be on November 15th. Wish you were coming. Our hotel dance will be on the 17th but I am not going to it. Between me and you, it's terrible although I gave them your name and others up there, so you will receive invitations to it if you haven't already.

Sorry, I didn't see Wash. Charlie had already told me he was home. He very seldom knows the whereabouts of his family.

So you still are a party girl. I bet you went to a nice little Halloween Party and ducked for apples or perhaps pinned the tail on the donkey.

The fair is all over until next year but I still can't get a seat when I get on the subway. There ain't no justice.

Well, my heart is still beating for you and I hope it is the same by you.

Please answer soon.

"Luke"

Wilkes-Barre
Nov. 12, 1939
Dear Luther,

Your letter was received and appreciated. Sara and I received invitations to something, sport dance, I gather. Is that the affair you were writing about?

I know you are busy attending formals galore. Well, have a fine time and think of me when you dance your favorite numbers.

Sara took us for a ride this morning. I had to get out of bed and go in my pajamas so she could get back in time for work. She's really coming on with her driving.

Can you imagine, Mrs. Barron, if you remember her, finally moved out of the hotel and, of all the jobs, she's keeping house for a priest in Berwick, taking Helen Louise with her. And that reminds me, Eddie Redington eloped and is not allowed to come back to the Hotel, exciting isn't it? The place must be a regular mausoleum now.

I'm trying to write you and listen to a Benny Goodman broadcast at the same time, the hard way.

Please take it easy, and keep your heart beating for me.
Mary

Hotel Wellington
Seventh Avenue
Fifty-Fifth and Fifty-Sixth Streets
New York

November 19, 1939
N.Y.C.

Dear Mary:

Your letter was highly appreciated and that is putting it mild. Write more soon, please.

I attended my first formal last Wednesday and it was nicely conducted. As you asked me, I thought of you when they played my favorite number but everyone was my favorite. I am hoping you can attend one or more of these lovely affairs before the season is completed. Please try.

You probably will receive a couple of invitations to dances but they will not be formals—not so hot.

Swell hearing of Sarah's automobile operating ability. Keep up the good work—tell her. When are you going to learn?

One never knows what is in store, referring to Mrs. Barron and Eddie Redington. More power to both of them.

Well, I am listening to some sweet music while writing your letter. It complements your charm perfectly.

"Luke"

Hotel Redington
Wilkes-Barre, Pa

November 24, 1939

Dear Luther,

It was so very nice to hear from you again. I enjoy each letter and the pleasure of reading them increases a thousand fold.

Did you spend a nice Thanksgiving? I thought of you while we were having dinner. Here's hoping you enjoyed yours as much as I did. It was grand knowing you enjoyed yourself at the dance. Maybe sometime I can attend one of those fine affairs before the season ends. At least I'll keep my fingers crossed.

Well, Sara took her test today and now she is a full-fledged driver. But I don't know when yours truly will follow through; it seems that I just can't get up the nerve to try. I'm a sissy I guess.

Wasn't it sad about poor Cleo. It seems too bad when one has to die at that age.

By the way, how are you coming on with the air-conditioning? I hope you are making fine progress, as I know you can.

Please give my very best regards to everyone especially Jocelyn. I've thought about her often lately.

Mary

Hotel Wellington
Seventh Avenue
Fifty-Fifth and Fifty-Sixth Streets
New York

Nov. 29, 1939
N.Y.C.
Dear Mary:

I've read your letter over repeatedly until I've learned it by heart. It helps so much.

I had Thanksgiving Dinner at the hotel. It was fair. Your thinking of me while you were eating tasted much better to me than the dinner I ate.

I saw Sis's boyfriend Harry. I don't think he got into school because of some complications.

There is a double crossing of fingers because mine are crossed in hopes of you attending a dance. Don't necessarily have to wait for a dance, you know.

Give Sarah a pat on the back for me, please. Come on Mary, what do you say—you're next.

I really have deep sympathy for Cleo Bunch. One never knows.

Thanks a million for asking about my air-conditioning training—coming along swell. Trying to continue.

I haven't seen Jocelyn for about two months. All others are well, also my babies. You know what I mean.*

Well I guess that is all the dirt for this time. I feel lonesome for you some time even though I do live in this big city.

Please answer soon.

"Luke"

My father is referring to his friends' babies.

Wilkes-Barre
Dec. 5, 1939
Dear Luther,

    I am so glad you enjoy these very humble missives of my composition. Sad as they are, I do mean well. I can assure you yours are equally enjoyed and I look forward to each one with utmost pleasure.

    I am so glad you are coming along with your air-conditioning training. By all means continue with the good work.

    Did I tell you that Harriet Oliver was here for the holiday? New York certainly has treated her rather hard. She said she came home for a rest. She should have taken a year.

    Mrs. Haley has been telling of her visit in the "Big Town." She was sorry to have missed you. I'll not forgive her. At least she could have told me how you looked or something.

    And really you have no conception of loneliness, believe me.

    My song these days is an old one "Honestly." It fits my mood perfectly.

Mary

Hotel Wellington
Seventh Avenue
Fifth-Fifth and Fifty-Sixth Streets
New York

December 11, 1939
N.Y.C.
Dear Mary:

Thanks again for your letter. Again, it was a pleasure to read it again and again.

Thanks again for your encouragement. I'll try hard to continue my studying.

I suppose you are being run ragged with the holiday shopping rush. Please be careful and don't over exert yourself and get plenty of rest.

As for myself, I have a lot of leisure time. Business is very slow so we are taking it rather easy until it picks up.

Dorothy the waitress asked about you and also asked me if you were coming down for the holidays. I would have liked to have told her yes but I gave her a sad <u>no</u>.

Incidentally, "Honestly" became my favorite song. Do you recall these words in the song—"I'm jealous of the moments I'm not with you."
"Luke"

The Letters

Wilkes-Barre, PA
December 18, 1939
Dear Luther,

    Your letters are still the sunshine in my life so don't ever stop writing and leave me in the dark.

    I have been very busy working overtime and everything else getting Kempton's ready for Christmas. Thank the gods it comes only once a year.

    Don't ever worry about me killing myself Christmas shopping. I never have been so lucky as to have so much to do. Nothing can hold you back like a limited budget.

    Andy has come home with some friends and intends to paint the town red. He's lucky if it will even turn pink!

    I don't think I've ever mentioned to you our Sadie Hawkins day club. Every Thursday we girls call on some fellow and let him pitch us a ball. It's lots of fun. We have bids a couple of weeks ahead of time. Better luck than the "SSS" club, remember it?

    Please give my best regards to Dorothy. Why didn't you tell her you were coming home for Christmas. I don't mind being surprised, really don't. My friends also ask if you are coming and I, too have to say a very sad no. You really should do something about it.
Mary

Hotel Wellington
Seventh Avenue
Fifty-Fifth and Fifty-Sixth Streets
New York

December 25, 1939
N.Y.C.

Dear Mary:

I trust that you and the family enjoyed a very Merry Christmas. Your sending those gloves was the most pleasant thing that happened to me this Christmas. Thanks a million but you always do and say the things that I like. I wonder why?

Yesterday (Sunday) I ate dinner at Champ's house. I had a swell time and enjoyed the dinner very much. Today (Christmas) I ate dinner with the Lawrences—also a tasty dinner but I derived most of my pleasure sitting in my little room writing this letter to you. These words are written as I would tell them to you face to face: Mary you are the most charming person I've ever met.

Wish Andy a Merry Christmas for me and I hope he doesn't run out of red paint.

I hope this Sadie Hawkins day club has a more successful existence than the S.S.S. Club. I don't want to feel slighted—I mean I want my turn when it's due. I'll be expecting to see the club call on me—don't forget.

Again, I want to thank you for your thoughtful present. Remember, it's the little things that mean so much.

Thank your Mother and Father for their greetings. I would like so much to see you but I just can't arrange to get time off right now. I wish so very much that I could.

Luke

P.S. I would like so very much to hear from you soon. Please and thank you. Happy New Year Dear.

The Letters

Wilkes-Barre, Pa
December 29, 1939
Dear Luther,

The nicest part of this whole holiday week was receiving your letter.

I want to thank you for the beautiful bag you sent me. I fell in love with it at first sight. You also know how my tastes run, strange isn't it.

I was so glad to hear that you enjoyed those fine dinners. It improved mine 100%. I had dinner at home Sunday and in Scranton Monday. Both were extra fine.

A new club in Scranton gave a semi-formal dance on Wednesday night. It was really very nice. I thought of you whenever they played a favorite number of mine, and that was often.

Have you heard about your cousin Paul? He became a bridegroom on Christmas day. It was truly a real surprise. Evelyn Payne also surprised us and became Mrs. Long on Sunday. The "bug" isn't losing a bit of time. So you be careful because I'm trusting you.

Well here's loads of luck for the New Year and please answer very soon.

Mary

1940

Nineteen forty was a historic year in African American history: Charles Drew created the first blood bank; Benjamin O. Davis Sr. became the first African American promoted to the rank of general in the U.S. Army; novelist Richard Wright's *Native Son* was published.

For my Luther and Mary, 1940 was a sad and ominous year—they faced more family deaths and the looming war.

On May 10, 1940, Hitler began to execute his plan for German domination of Europe. German forces invaded the Netherlands, Belgium, and Luxembourg, as well as France. With German encouragement, the Soviet Union occupied the Baltic states [Estonia, Latvia, and Lithuania] in June and formally annexed them in August 1940. Italy, a member of the Axis (countries allied with Germany), also joined the war in June. It was time for the U.S. to begin preparation for possible entry into the European war.

On September 16th 1940, Congress passed the Burke-Wadsworth Act, and the Selective Service, commonly called the *draft*, was born. All men between the ages of 21 and 36 were required to register. The first draftees were selected on October 29th. Secretary of War Henry L. Stimson drew draft numbers out of a glass bowl and handed them to President Roosevelt. The President read them aloud to the nation. There were 20 million eligible men but nearly half were rejected the first year, either for health reasons or illiteracy.

The Letters

Hotel Wellington
Seventh Avenue
Fifty-Fifth and Fifty-Sixth Streets
New York

January 3, 1940
N.Y.C.
Dear Mary:

So pleased to hear that you enjoyed your Christmas, and also my little gift—you know your pleasure is my happiness.

Chris spent Tuesday evening with me. We exchanged ideas and talked about the past and present—just a general gab session.

Several people have asked about you again. I'm always delighted to tell them what I can about you—Mrs. Boone, Jocelyn, John, Champ and his Mrs. See, you are in demand here so you better get hep to yourself.

A new club—so you all have increased your social area in other words you all are spreading out and doing things.

I went to see Emily and I was informed that she was up there. She will tell me about Paul and his new bride when she returns. Congrats to Evelyn.

I want to thank you for your visit to New York this past summer. Also your wonderful letters and the fact that I know you. Just a summary of the past year's pleasure I've gotten through knowing you and I hope to enjoy even more this year.

I'm elated to know that you are trusting in me and I'll make every effort to live up to your expectations—so help me.

Well, that is all for this time but you know I want to hear from you soon.
"Luke"

January 8, 1940
Wilkes-Barre, Penna
Dear Luther,

Your letter was read and reread. The pleasure of receiving them has never waned.

Emily and I had a gab session of our own practically everyday since she's been home. Mrs. Haley is very sick so I guess Emily will be here quite a while. I was surprised to see Llewellyn yesterday. They said that Clarence had just gone so I didn't see him.

Did you have a nice New Year? Ours was very quiet. I went to two shows and afterwards Emily, Paul and our family were up at the Sand's. The wine was good so what more could we want. I was very careful, I took only one glass. I gave up long ago trying to take two glasses of anything.

It is very nice of your friends to ask of me now and then and please remember to give them my regards and I think of them often in our moments of reminiscing.

I've enjoyed the utmost pleasure being in your company during the past year and I hope to enjoy just as much or even more this year. I'm going to jump very salty if you don't try to come home more often and I mean it.

Listen to "Darn that Dream" and answer soon. Mary

Hotel Wellington
Seventh Avenue
Fifty-Fifth and Fifty-Sixth Streets
New York

January 15, 1940
N.Y.C.
Dear Mary:

I derived the usual thrill of reading your very well penmanship and composition, please do it again.

I hope that Mrs. Haley is better. I'm sure everything is being done to assure her recovery. So you and Emily have been doing a little "around the town." So you've limited your drinking to one, very good idea I must say. A little is better than too much.

I met Blanche and Olan on New Year's Eve. They were looking for excitement and I was trying to duck it as much as possible. So goes it—one is never satisfied. I worked New Year's Eve—had lots of fun at work. Drunks by the score—male, female, old and young. The best part of the evening was going home.

Listen, there'll be no getting salty. I'm trying to get some time as soon as possible. Hold tight. Listen for "All the Things You Are."
"Luke"

This letter introduces Skippy, the Brooks family dog.

January 23, 1940
Wilkes-Barre
Dear Luther,

It was so nice to have heard from you again. This cold weather is certainly getting me down and a letter from you now and then helps me to keep a normal temperature. They're my anti-freeze if you get what I mean.

Like a crazy nit-wit I went riding in a rumble seat last week and now I've been in a couple of days with a bad cold. There was no one to lend me an extra coat and so I suffer.

I haven't seen Emily for a while but my mother says that Mrs. Haley is just the same. The doctors still say she has little chance of recovery. She hasn't moved or talked since right after New Year's. Sonny is just as bad as ever. Emily has a hard time keeping him quiet. Every once and a while, she sends him over to our house, but he and Skippy don't get along so well. I guess our Skippy is spoiled too.

Louise Downey spent last week-end with us. Her mother is living with Elwood, in, I think, Syracuse. Louise is thinking of going to live with Wash in Rochester. I'd forgotten that he was there he moves so much.

Well so much for now—take care of yourself in this cold weather.
Mary

The Letters

My father's aunt, known to all as Mrs. Haley, died as a result of a stroke on January 24th, 1940. This letter is written a few days after my father returned to New York City following the funeral.

Hotel Wellington
Seventh Avenue
Fifty-Fifth and Fifty-Sixth Streets
New York

January 29, 1940
N.Y.C.

Dear Mary:

Have arrived back in the turmoil of the city. For some reason, it was no thrill returning.

I suppose I took advantage of your good nature and kept you up late, but I really did appreciate your charming presence, your smiling countenance, and your tender caresses, and you make me feel that it's a wonderful world.

Do you suppose if I make a special trip back next week, Sis would go up to 318 with me, but she must stay until 4 a.m. and keep dad waiting. <u>ha! ha! ha!</u>

She doesn't mind if I have a little laugh on her I hope. She can have one on me some day.

Hope your mother doesn't have any more of those dreadful attacks again. It gave me the jitters for a while. All of you be very careful.

Tell Emily if you see her that I'll be up Sunday afternoon.

Thank you again for dinner. Your cooking or even your effort is good enough for me.

Faithful to you
"Luke"

Wilkes-Barre, PA
February 4, 1940
Dear Luther,

It was so very nice having you here for four very short days. I hate to return to writing letters again, they somehow seem so inadequate and I'd much rather talk to you. Since I can't talk, I'll just keep on writing.

I didn't in the least little bit mind staying up late with you. I only regret I have so few opportunities of doing so.

I was positively overwhelmed to receive a short but sweet letter from Jocelyn last week. Thank her for dropping us a line when you see her and tell her I will reciprocate in the near future.

We were sorry to see Emily and Sonny leave but I know she was glad to get home and rest. She certainly needs it.

Parran Foster and Alice Porter were married on Thursday night. They have my best wishes, etc.

Since there really isn't anything more in the lines of news that I know of, I'll just sign off here.

Please answer very, very soon because I miss you very much.

Mary

Hotel Wellington
Seventh Avenue
Fifty-Fifth and Fifty-Sixth Streets
New York

Feb. 9, 1940
N.Y.C.

Dear Mary:

So sorry I could not prolong my short stay when I was in town. My being near and with you has always touched me deeply. I must admit that I am weak for your invincible charm and each time it gets stronger—so fine!

We have taken serious steps to see what we can do for you and Sarah in the line of employment in the city. We, meaning Martha Moore, Emily and myself. Emily told or rather asked Martha to keep the look-out for you. I hope we can do something for you and I hope very much the next time you come down, it would be a good idea to put applications in at a number of different stores and what not. The sooner the better you know.

Haven't seen Jocelyn yet, we seldom see each other but when I do I shall relay your shock.

Add my very best wishes, etc. to yours for the newly weds. May there be more happy marriages to speak of.

If I remember correctly, Saturday is the day of Andy and his gang to invade the old town. Why not go out and have a real good time with them? I much rather hear of you enjoying yourself than the usual boring complaints about W-B that I have heard.

The end has come but just a brief intermission. I am waiting for an answer soon.

"Luke"

My father's Uncle Harry died on February 7, 1940.

The "Kraft Music Hall" was a radio program that aired on NBC's radio network from the mid-1930's to the late 1940's. For many of those years, Bing Crosby was the host.

Wilkes-Barre
Feb. 15, 1940
Dear Luther,

Thank you so much for the lovely Valentine greetings. You were very sweet to send them and I loved every word of it.

Sarah and I appreciate very much all of your interest in trying to locate us in your city. I hope that we will be able to come in the near future. But we know that all of this takes time. You see my mother and father refuse to allow us to leave home and to look out for something ourselves. They seem to think we are incapable of taking care of ourselves or even thinking like grown people. We get terribly put out about it, but that is the most we can do, I guess. Parents are possessed with the most stubborn wills, so I've discovered. They just won't give in until they have to.

I was very sorry to hear of your uncle's death. It seems it never rains unless it pours.

We went to the dance and reception given by the "Y" for Andy's gang. Brud Holland is really a charming personality and I enjoyed meeting him. Ben Johnson was also here so that made it unanimous. Contrary to my expectations we had a fine time and I was glad that I went. (The party was at Wilmer's).

Give my regards to everyone and tell Emily not to worry about her father, he is coming along fine except for being a little lonesome and that will pass I hope.

Answer real soon.
Mary
P. S. Enjoyed Bing Crosby singing "If I Knew Then What I Know Now"

The Letters

Hotel Wellington
Seventh Avenue
Fifty-Fifth and Fifty-Sixth Streets
New York

Feb. 22, 1940
N.Y.C.
Dear Mary:

Very pleased to hear that you enjoyed my humble Valentine greeting. Every word was a true sentiment.

Emily and I were talking about Sarah and you to-day, merely checking up on each other. We earnestly would like both of you to get located as soon as possible, of course you know how I feel about it.

Thanks for your sympathy of my uncle's death. I hope my mother is taking it easy.

So pleased to know that you enjoyed yourself and also to know that you met some interesting persons. Meeting people does break the monotony of seeing the same faces each and every day. Perhaps that is why I had to leave. I didn't want you to become bored with me while each time I see you I become more interested.

I can't believe that you have acknowledged the fact that Bing Crosby's singing ability reached your approval—bravo! It took time but I suppose you are convinced. Incidentally, the number is quite appropriate, I think. More next time.
"Luke"

Wilkes-Barre, Pa
February 28, 1940
Dear Luther,

So nice to have heard from you again. Your letters and spring are all that I look for.

We have been having a real social season here lately. We play pinochle and Monopoly at first one home and then the other trying to make this darn old winter pass quickly.

I suppose the team will be there this week-end to play basketball. I hope they have a more successful game than last year. If you attend maybe their luck will change, don't forget.

Listen, Luther, I don't like you writing such things as my being bored with you. I can't conceive of the idea of anything so impossible. I have an absolutely one track mind. It just doesn't change—remember that. That is really a poor excuse for your staying away any how.

Your mother is quite all right. Naturally, she was upset for a while, but I think she will be o.k.

How is Emily? I hope she is feeling much better... Please give her my very best regards.

Keep well and write soon.

Mary

P.S. I'm going to see "Eternally Yours" with Sis and Mother. Sis says she is waiting for you to take her to "318". She has been coming home early and she misses the early morning serenade from Dad.

The Letters

Hotel Wellington
Seventh Avenue
Fifty-Fifth and Fifty-Sixth Streets
New York

March 5, 1940
N.Y.C.
Dear Mary:

First, I am so sorry for saying that I was afraid of becoming a bore. I won't say it again, honest. Nice reading your letter regardless.

I even kept score for the team and still they didn't win, although they played a fairly good game. The score was twenty-five to thirty-nine. They are an entertaining bunch if not athletic. Some of them went to the Golden Gate Saturday night. Of course, I was with them. We walked in like Cox's army.

Bill [Grimes] replenished his supply of big hats. I also took him downtown to purchase other commodities. I suppose he will display them for you.

Do you suppose if I should sponsor an expedition up in those parts I could bag some wild bears. There is a rumor that hunting wild game is very promising in that section. Please inform me to that point. Be careful you are not attacked, but I suppose you are well-armed when you leave the house.

On Friday afternoon (Feb. 23) I went out and carelessly left my door open, as I always have, and when I returned I discovered two of my best suits missing. Yes, I was robbed of my black suit which I just got less than two months ago and my green one less than a year ago. Who ever did it was quite choicey in picking because they left me the oldest ones.

Mrs. Lawrence was very swell and considerate and immediately began to check up on the other tenants in the house, but no success so far. The value of the two suits together constituted about 65 dollars. She told me not to pay any rent until I replaced one of them. Please don't tell my mother or anyone who might know her. She has enough worries.

It seems as though since the beginning of this year I have received bad news and gotten bad luck at times. I felt very despondent and often thought that if I could just hold your hand it would've been great relief. It's the price you pay for being careless. Although I have felt like just giving up everything.

I think of you and our love that I can look forward to, that feeling is automatically erased from my mind, thanks to you. My trip home in January was a mournful one, but I derived considerable amount of pleasure seeing my folks and spending those few hours with you. But better days are coming, so I'll keep my chin up. I felt that you should know what happens to me whether good, bad, or indifferent.

I trust that your mother, Sis and yourself enjoyed "Eternally Yours". You may tell Sis that I shall graciously accept her invitation to her favorite night club "318" if and when I come home. The serenade, as you called it, will be entirely on me.

I told Emily you often ask about her—she returns the same to you. Well I guess that is all the dirt for this time.

The reason I don't come home often is because I thought I was a bore. I'm just a bad fellow, huh, Mary? Now you've got to tell me you care again. I guess I kinda like it. *ha! ha!*

Do not hesitate to answer soon. It's a blue world without you. "Luke"

The Letters

Wilkes-Barre, Pa
March 11, 1940
Dear Luther,

 I was terribly sorry to hear of your loss. I hope by now that you have some recompense. Mrs. Lawrence was really very sweet and considerate. But, Luther, I can't imagine you being so careless; this should be a good lesson for you (consider yourself properly reprimanded.) I do wish I could have been there to offer a little consolation. But I'll make up for all of this when the time arrives.

 I haven't as yet seen any of the boys who were on the team. But with you keeping score for them they could have done better than that.

 What in the world are you getting at by the wild game hunting? I haven't heard anything of that either. Could have been eaten up alive, thanks for warning me.

 Your mother was over the other day. She is looking much better now. So you don't have to worry about her. Tell Emily, too, that her dad is still coming along. He washes every week as regular as a clock. He gave some kind of a supper last week which was a success.

 Have you heard of Mr. Rasper's death. I don't know what is the matter with everybody in this town, but they certainly are beginning this year all wrong. It is really very depressing. He was the third person to die here last week. I didn't know the other two but they were old residents. But here's hoping for a brighter future.

 Please don't let yourself feel depressed. This bad luck can't last. How can I be happy when I know you feel bad. Thank you so much for wanting me to share troubles and happiness and I hope that I can always be a consolation to you, Luther.

 And you know, of course, that I care, silly.

 Please answer real soon.

Mary

Hotel Wellington
Seventh Avenue
Fifty-Fifth and Fifty-Sixth Streets
New York

March 18, 1940
N.Y.C.
Dear Mary:

Many thanks for your sincere sympathy. It was very soothing and advisable.

If and when you see Bill, tell him I received his letter and thank him for it. Please.

I was referring to the two bears that escaped from one of the theatres a couple of weeks ago when I mentioned the hunting, etc. It was in the New York papers in case you didn't know it. I was certain you knew about it.

Thanks for the news of my mother. By the way, how has yours been doing, also the rest of the family, including Skippy. Emily is going to write you, she said.

Sorry to hear of Mr. Rasper's death. Death seems to play a large role in that vicinity this year. I hope it has ceased for a while.

Well Mary, spring is coming, you know so I've got to act and feel accordingly. Don't worry there will be no poetry.

Well, nothing further but please answer soon because I feel about your letters as you feel about mine.
"Luke"

The Letters

Wilkes-Barre, Pa
March 26, 1940
Dear Luther,

    I hope you spent a most enjoyable Easter. Mine was fair. I think I'll spend the rest of the week in recuperation. I suppose you led the Easter Parade. It was much too cold for me. I gladly stuck to my red flannels, etc.

    Louise Downey spent a few days here before leaving for Rochester to live with Wash. Can you imagine him settled and keeping house? Believe me, I can't. He and Will have been shopping for furniture etc. so he must be quite domesticated, more power to him.

    I can hardly write. My dad is actually <u>running</u> around playing with Skippy who, by the way is still the craziest one in our family. Who would have thought a dog could have worked so much change. Because next to Sarah, my dad is the very slowest person I know.

    My mother received a letter from Emily, last week. She wrote of Sonny's killer-diller tie—some fellow that Sonny.

    Have you discovered anything concerning the disappearance of your suits—I hope that you have.

    Well, I've bored you long enough with this idle chatter. I'll call it a day.

    Listen to "Faithful to You" and think of me.
Mary

Hotel Wellington
Seventh Avenue
Fifty-Fifth and Fifty-Sixth Streets
New York

April 2, 1940
N.Y.C.
Dear Mary:

Gosh, I hope you all aren't washed away. From the newspapers and radio news broadcasts, W-B has turned into Venice or perhaps a repetition of the Johnstown flood. You all are trying to make history. But, I do hope you are safe and sound. Be sure the boat doesn't leak when you go out in it.

Those were mighty pretty words on that card you sent me. They helped much in the realization of it being Easter. Otherwise it was just another Sunday for me. I have you to thank once again.

Your father is just getting his second childhood. Don't hold it against him.

That's swell news about Wash…hope he has the best of luck in his ordeal.

Nothing further on the loss of my clothes. I've just given them up as a loss.

Well I hope you all survive the havoc. I suppose the situation is well in hand so I'll will say
Au revoir
"Luke"

April 8, 1940
Wilkes-Barre, Pa
Dear Luther,

What have you been doing with yourself these fine spring days? I hope they haven't kept you working nights all this time. That would be terrible.

Your girlfriend went out in the rain last week without rubbers etc. and now she's suffering with a terrific sore throat and a bad cold. It seems that I can't get rid of it. Well any how I got a couple of days off from work. Some comfort in that anyhow.

Of the flood—hasn't been as bad as it was reported. Hate to disappoint you but I didn't even see a boat. Between you and me this entire "burg" could go down the river and there'd be no regrets. But so far there is little danger of that.

Bill Grimes informed me last night that you had been very sweet as to send us another copy of the "Downbeat", but so far he had completely forgotten to deliver it. Thank you and when it is delivered, I know we'll enjoy reading it. One must keep up the latest in all things.

Andy was here with another fellow from Lincoln over the week-end. That fellow is crazier than a lunatic. Between him and Sara, you've never heard such crazy talk. Andy keeps coming back so he must like it.

So much for this time. Answer real soon and give my regards to everyone.

Mary

P.S. If you were here to come see me, this cold would be a thousand times improved.

Hotel Wellington
Seventh Avenue
Fifty-Fifth and Fifty-Sixth Streets
New York

April 16, 1940
N.Y.C.

Dear Mary:

Spring has just gotten me woozie, if you know what I mean, because I don't. I heard some one say it so I'm telling you too. I hope you are jelling in accordance with the weather.

I don't work nights any more, thank you. It really doesn't matter how I work so long as you are not here.

Gosh, you are very careless with yourself, venturing out into that damp, wet weather without the proper equipment. How do you expect me to worry about you and take care of myself too? Don't do that. Please feel better for me.

So glad to receive true report of the flood area. All that I read and heard on the radio was very severe, in fact, gave me the creeps. Your attitude about the burg is striking. Should the whole burg, as you called it, went down the river where should I find you when I look for you?

So very sorry you were not here the last week or so because I had the good fortune of seeing Fred Allen and the Hit Parade broadcasts. But when you come down this summer, that is I hope, perhaps, I can get some tickets although they are hard to procure.

That guy Andy just comes home whenever the mood strikes him and he can get a companion to accompany him, doesn't he. Of course he'll always come back to see so glamorous a person as your sister Sara. She is also so amusing. Don't tell her I said so though, please.

Incidentally, because of the fair this year or summer, I should say, we must take our vacations early. Mine is from May 3rd until the 10th providing they don't change it. My problem is should I stay here and take it easy for that week or come home.

I'm open for suggestions. I'll be glad if you would offer yours. Thank you. My next letter will be more definite so answer soon.

"I'm So Romantic" by the way is my favorite number so beware.
"Luke"

Hotel Redington
Absolutely Fireproof
Wilkes-Barre, PA

April 22, 1940

Dear Luther,

It was so nice to have heard from you once more. Also to know that you have effectively welcomed spring. We have something in common.

If you give another thought to any place except Wilkes-Barre for your vacation I'll be the saltiest lass on two continents, <u>no</u> fooling. How could you even suggest taking it easy in New York or an alternative? I'll certainly remember to speak to you about that, so help me.

Andy, bless his heart, invited a crowd of us to another "frat" dance at Lincoln. But unfortunately nobody was able to attend it. He was very disappointed and a friend of his wrote that he was quite angry. We really feel terrible ourselves, after all, we were the losers of what could have been a grand week-end.

And that reminds me, Rudy Andruz was here last Thursday night. It was his first visit home since he left last summer.

I guess that is all there for now. Oh! Yes, my cold has disappeared and I feel fine. Thank you.

Please let me know your plans real soon.

Mary

Hotel Wellington
Seventh Avenue
Fifty-Fifth and Fifty-Sixth Streets
New York

April 30, 1940
N.Y.C.

Dear Mary,

I received your letter and really appreciate your suggesting that I come home. If you can take it I can. I'll keep you up very late and no yawning. I won't be home on 3rd. It has been detained one week later or the 10th instead. You have longer to rest now, so take advantage of it.

You don't treat poor Andy with fairness. I'm sure he was mortified because of your nonappearance, there ain't no justice.

So pleased to hear of your cold disappearing, continue to keep well. Understand.

Incidentally, listen to "Ask-It-Basket" over W.A.B.C. Thursday night at 8:00 Daylight saving time. I sent a question in for that program. Perhaps they will not use it, but I won't be able to hear it. I hope it will not inconvenience you. Let me know if they use it, please.

Well I guess they will not change my vacation date again, but will let you know in case they do.

Answer soon.

Luke

Wilkes-Barre, Pa
May 6, 1940
Dear Luther,

I won't say I was glad to hear from you because I would much rather have seen you. How dare you build me up for such a let down? Please don't disappoint me this time, I can't take it, really I can't.

Chris was over here over the weekend. He said that he had been to see you, but as usual you weren't around. I told him not to tell me such things. I don't like to hear them. You know, what you don't know doesn't hurt you, does it?

How are Emily and Sonny and everyone else? I know they are all making the most of this spring weather. Believe me, I am.

Mary Buster was here over the week-end, she was expecting to see you. You can't imagine how disappointed she was. I told her not to come next week because I would be too busy to entertain her. But Mary just can't take a hint so I guess she'll be here as usual.

Remember, I'll be looking for you so please try and make it this time.

Mary

P.S. Don't forget to write in any case. Please. MEB

The Letters

Hotel Wellington
Seventh Avenue
Fifty-Fifth and Fifty-Sixth Streets
New York

May 8, 1940
N.Y.C.

Dear Mary:

I'll see you Friday evening!

Whooppee!

Luke

Hotel Wellington
Seventh Avenue
Fifth-Fifth and Fifty-Sixth Streets
New York

May 20, 1940
N.Y.C.
Dear Mary:

I am very grateful to you for those swell evenings we spent, frankly I could use more of them. You were very sweet as I expected before I came home. I hope you will recuperate soon. I'm a bad boy, aren't I?

All of you were very, very swell and made my visit most enjoyable.

You must convey my thanks to Adrian for the part she played also. By all means my regards to your friend Lucy. She is the working girls companion.*

I told Emily, Mrs. Lawrence, Champ and everybody about you. I must tell someone of your charms. I'll be waiting to see you and I mean it.

Well it's Monday morning so I guess I'll gather the laundry up for the Chinamen. Darn it. Well, so goes it.

Chris came by the hotel Sunday night to receive the news. He may be up soon, he said.

Well I guess that will be all until the next installment. I'll be waiting for your answer.

"Luke"

P.S. You were marvelous!!!

Adrienne (correct spelling) was Mary's manager and Lucy was one of her co-workers.

The Letters

Wilkes-Barre, Pa
May 26, 1940
Dear Luther,

First I want you to know how very much I enjoyed your brief stay with us. It seemed that I was celebrating my vacation too just knowing you were coming up each evening. I really felt badly when it was all over.

I have recuperated fully from the late hours. And you were a very bad boy, believe me. You'll be my downfall yet.

I don't know what happened but I am listening to Jack Benny in the middle of the afternoon. I am shamelessly writing to you while still donned in my sleeping apparel. I hope no one drops in, they'll most certainly get a shock when they gaze at me.

Lucy and all the girls send their regards. They've been worried to death all week because I haven't written to you sooner. They made me promise solemnly to write to-day. Poor Lucy met with a serious accident on Tuesday. She stepped in a bowl of soup cooling on their cellar steps and was nearly killed. Her head was cut and her back is a solid bruise. But she managed to pull thru and feels quite herself. I told her to be careful. She aged ten years in a few days of hobbling around.

I've been reading "Native Son" and am quite convinced I don't care for Chicago. It was certainly a startling tale.

Listen to "Where Was I". It leaves me breathless.

<u>Write soon</u>
Mary
<u>You were sort of extra special yourself</u>

Hotel Wellington
Seventh Avenue
Fifty-Fifth and Fifty-Sixth Streets
New York

May 31, 1940
N.Y.C.

Dear Mary:

So pleased with your missive and also to know that you appreciated my coming home. It was really swell. After returning here the anxiety to want to repeat those evenings grew feverish. I admit I was bad but under the circumstances I couldn't be bad by myself. It is not my desire to be your downfall, I'm more inclined to idolize you—you know you're my extraordinary girl.

To be remembered by such a host of charm is more than I can believe. Please express my gratitude to Lucy and others. Please tell Lucy to be more soup careful.

I hope "Native Son" didn't contaminate your clean mind but after all I shouldn't think of you as weak.

It is Friday morning and my day off and it is raining to beat the blazes, so to appease my mind I'm writing you this letter. You are a consolation to me although we are miles apart. You're dynamite when you're near me. Incidentally, please send the stamps back to me from each letter that I send from now on. I am getting some new stamps to add to my scant collection. Since the war, I don't get foreign stamps, so I'll just be content with U.S. stamps until....

Thank you, my dear....

Well, I guess the end has come until next time. I'll be waiting for your answer soon <u>please</u>.

You listen for "Imagination." You are so wonderful.

"Luke"

The Letters

Perhaps my mother was prompted to read "Gone with the Wind" because of Hattie McDaniel's Oscar win at the 1940 Academy Awards for her portrayal of Mammy. Though set against the backdrop of the Civil War from a Southern viewpoint, my mother enjoyed Scarlett O'Hara and Rhett Butler's romance.

Wilkes-Barre, Pa
June 6, 1940
Dear Luther,

Your very sweet letter was most appreciated. I read it um-teen times and enjoyed every word. But it would be so much nicer if you were here. You can't imagine how I miss your badness. I'll never be the same, really I won't and it's all your fault! You shouldn't love and leave me like you do.

I've just spent practically two weeks reading "Gone with the Wind." It was one of the most enjoyable books I've ever read. I am sorrier than ever to have missed the picture. I'll bet Clark Gable (my favorite actor—he's got hair on his chest) was a killer-diller Rhett Butler. I get weak thinking about it. Wooooooooo!

How are Emily, Sonny, and the rest of the family and all of our friends? You haven't mentioned them for such a long time. Please give them my regards, I don't want them to forget me.

You see I didn't forget the stamps. In fact I remember everything that you tell me so be careful what you say.

Please answer very, very soon and I'll be waiting to hear from you.
Mary
"Imagination" is also one of my very best favorite. *MEB*

Hotel Wellington
Seventh Avenue
Fifty-Fifth and Fifty-Sixth Streets
New York

June 12, 1940
N.Y.C.

Dear Mary:

So sorry your letter had an ending because that means the finish. Try writing an endless letter next time.

I haven't seen "Gone with the Wind" either so we both still can see it. All you have to do is come to New York. Isn't that simple enough? Try it. Gable is one of my favorite actors also, of course Bing's another. By the way I have hair on my chest also, you don't need a microscope to see it either. I'll let you see it when you come down. Perhaps I'm getting a little Gablish.

Every one of your friends and admirers are asking about you and inquire as to when you'll be down. You must tell me what to tell them.

Very grateful for the stamps. Please send all of the stamps. Just pull the stamp off the letter.

So you remember everything I told you. That's why I told you those things, dear. I'm waiting to receive your letter soon.

"Luke"

Wilkes-Barre, Pa
June 18, 1940
Dear Luther,

I'd like very much to write an endless letter to you, but as it is I have to struggle with my imagination to write an ordinary letter. Suppose you try, I love receiving such from you. I'll spend the rest of my life reading it.

I am sorry I can't say definitely when my vacation will be so that you could inform your friends. I am rather worried myself. If these wars keep on this way I won't need a vacation. I'll be too busy saying "bon voyage" to all of you fellows, but I do hope not. Everything seems to be happening with such rapidity that one hardly knows what one will be doing next week.

Maude Roach was here last week. It was her first visit home since her marriage. She told us about not going to see her while we were in N.Y. and made us promise to do so on our next trip. Don't you let me forget, please.

Poor Andy came home from school after a week's delay. He didn't graduate as he expected (his French) so I guess he rather hated it; he did brag a little, you know Andy. Our friend Harold bought himself a Packard. I haven't seen it yet but he said it was the wreck of 1890 or something. He's keeping it up in the country.

Well that seems to be all the news there is right now, except that I still miss you very, very much. Write me <u>soon</u>, please.
Mary
P.S. Listen for my song, "I Can't Resist You." It's true too.
Also your stamp

Hotel Wellington
Seventh Avenue
Fifty-Fifth and Fifty-Sixth Streets
New York

June 23, 1940
N.Y.C.

Dear Mary:

I hadn't thought much of the war because I've be spending my time thinking of you. Although it is a quite a swift ordeal. I suppose before this letter reaches you, Hitler will be here for me. He's a louse, isn't he.

Well, since you don't know the exact date of your vacation, I can at least look forward to your coming. If you shouldn't come, you will be committing an injustice to me. The same goes for you as went for me.

Sorry to hear of Andy's misfortune and glad to hear of Harold's good fortune or is it good. I'll take you to see Maude if you know where she lives. I'm sure I don't!

It's strange that when ever I hear music I automatically think of you. I'll bet any living human I got the sweetest girl friend in the whole world. I'll see even go so far as to bet you. Is there any reason why I'm so anxious to want to see you. Please remind your manager of your vacation, you know she may have forgotten it. Wake her up to the fact. You know this is a serious matter and has to be dealt with care so you just give her a good shaking—please.

"You're Just an Angel in Disguise," [is] mine too!
"Luke"

The Letters

June 28, 1940
Wilkes-Barre
Dear Luther,

You make me feel I can hardly wait for my vacation, writing such sweet letters. Adrienne hasn't as yet made up her mind concerning my vacation, she is so busy planning her own. But she has not forgotten, I'd never let her do that. I expect it will be the end of July or the middle of August. Either before she goes or when she returns.

We're going to a dance in Scranton tonight. It's been so long since I've attended any kind of an affair that I've forgotten how to act. I'll just sit out and think of you and have a most enjoyable evening.

It seems that Wilkes-Bare is haunted. Ethel Wilson is very ill. They don't expect her to live. Her lungs are completely gone, and this poor girl never even guessed such a thing. It's frightening really, you never know what is in store for you.

Poor me, a mosquito bit me two weeks ago on the arm. It was so sore that I went to a doctor Wednesday and found I had an abscess. Now I'm taking cod liver oil. My dad insisted and I hate it. There just doesn't seem to be any justice.

Now you know everything so I guess I'll just close until the next time.

Please answer <u>very</u>, <u>very</u> soon.
Mary

Hotel Wellington
Seventh Avenue
Fifty-Fifth and Fifty-Sixth Streets
New York

July 5, 1940
N.Y.C.
Dear Mary:

Six wild girls invaded N.Y.C. last week-end. They seemed to enjoy every minute of their short stay. I couldn't keep up with them. None of them were supposed to be married and they had any number of fellows come to see them in that short stay.

They sold the idea of picnic going to them also. They have been planning for it although that is all the further it may go.

I suppose I won't expect to see you until after the picnic. I'm saving my funniest fun, my heartiest laughs, and most pleasant smiles for you and with you.

I had a surprise visit from Maude and her sister Helen Tuesday morning. I really didn't recognize her sister. They gave me the address and insisted that I come up before she returns. But I am so busy I don't know if I can or not, although I told them I would.

I hope your system used at the dance was successful and you enjoyed yourself. Very, very sorry to hear of Ethel's death. It really hurts to hear of a young person's death.

That's one advantage in New York. We do not have any mosquitoes. Cod liver oil is a builder-upper and you know that is what I want you to be. Dad knows best. Hello to the family.
"Luke"

The Letters

Wilkes-Barre, Pa
July 12, 1940
Dear Luther,

 Every time I sit down to write to you I feel a little bluer. Your vacation seems to have been at least ten years ago, so slowly does time pass for me.

 Those six wild girls came home raving of the ball they pitched. For once, we're content to listen. Always when it's about N.Y.

 Thank you, I had an enjoyable time at the dance. As usual I thought of you.

 We were surprised last Saturday to see Emily and Sonny. Paul and Mr. Haley don't know how to act having a woman in the house again. And men say they can get along without women.

 My vacation comes the week of August 11th so please save everything for me. But really, Luther, I still feel that you will be getting tired of my coming to N.Y. It seems every time you turn around, I'm there. And I will keep you up late in spite of all the good resolutions I make. My will power is weak where you're concerned.

 Well, I'll have to close because "I've got a date with a memory tonight." (My favorite number now.)
Mary

Hotel Wellington
Seventh Avenue
Fifty-Fifth and Fifty-Sixth Streets
New York

July 19, 1940
N.Y.C.

Dear Mary:

Swell to hear you enjoyed yourself at the dance in Scranton. You know your pleasure is my happiness.

Emily and Sonny didn't do me justice. I went to pay them my weekly visit when I was informed that they had escaped to hometown. I hope they are enjoying themselves, at the least.

Very excellent news, your vacation, it's about time. So you come to N.Y. once a year for a short week and you come too often? You know I should get mad and make you stay down here when you come. Did you say I get tired of seeing you? Well have you a song to go with that? I have and it is "All My Time is Yours." That's one they haven't recorded yet. As far as being weak, the feeling is mutual. Do you dig me?

I saw Jocelyn and spilled the news to her. She was very pleased. She also asked if Sarah was coming with you of course, which I didn't know. I think I can stand her if she wishes to come with you. I suppose Emily will be back by then.

As you ask for everything, well that is your legal right—my all! Do you dig me?

My secretary has type-written some literature about your President F.D.R. I hope you enjoy it. Enclosed you will find a copy. The reason my secretary does not type write your letter is because I can't let him get into my precious business. Do you_____?

Waiting for your answer so please don't keep me waiting too long.

Have your heard "I'll Never Smile Again" by Tommy Dorsey? By all means, hear it.

"Luke"

P.S. Please take it easy at the picnic. The boys may be up.

My father's typewritten note was not in the envelope in which his handwritten letter was mailed. From my mother's salutation, I assume my father signed the typed note Clark Gable or some other well-known movie star.

July 26, 1940
Wilkes-Barre
Dear "Hollywood,"

So you've been holding out on me! This was the first time I had heard of your new name and I trusted you to tell everything.

It was really swell having all the fellows here for the picnic. I do hope they enjoyed themselves as much as we did. But we were really ashamed of your people. They really tried to show their worst last night. Andy and Harold are really a disgrace to the community. And my mother wonders why we never invite anybody to Wilkes-Barre. Well she certainly knows now, believe me. In spite of all of the contention, though I really enjoyed having them here and I hope they come again.

Luther, you can't imagine how thrilled I was over the telephone conversation last night. It was a most wonderful and unexpected pleasure, I assure you. I am sorry I couldn't hear so well but the Coaster and the falls over the land were really too much competition.

Mr. Liebowitz came in from New York and informed us that we have to take two weeks vacation. One with pay and one without. So my first week begins on the 29th and since I hadn't time to make any plans I shall make it a leisurely one at home and will I appreciate the rest, so help me.

I am surprised at you not knowing that Emily was home. She only stayed here one week. I hope by now you have been to see her. I imagine she is rather blue. At least she left us that way.

The Letters

Well, Luther, I listened to your song and it left me breathless. Champ says that I can come to his house and play it as much as I care to and I intend to wear it out.

Well it's bed time so I'll just say good-night and please answer very, very soon.

Mary

Please forgive this stationary, it's all I have.

Hotel Wellington
Seventh Avenue
Fifty-Fifth and Fifty-Sixth Streets
New York

July 29, 1940
N.Y.C.

Dear Mary:

So happy to learn that you have two weeks vacation. I don't see why you don't spend both weeks here. All you have to do is get here. You have nothing further to worry about, even if you wanted to stay a month. Leave that to me.

Furthermore, I have quite a few nice friends for you to meet and if you come earlier and stay longer we can eliminate that week of rushing hither and thither. You can't let me down since you have the time available, please come sooner. Emily will be glad to have you, I'm sure. I shall tell her you will arrive soon, now you can't have me telling her a lie. Tell me when you are arriving so I can make arrangements to meet you, so your next letter will have that information.

Will expect to hear from you soon.

Luke

The Letters

July 30, 1940
Wilkes-Barre
Dear Luther,

You're really awfully sweet to want me to come to NY for two weeks. I can't tell you how awfully much I'd love to come; but you see my vacation is split. A week now and then on the 11th of August I get another week. It's really disgusting but since they are all this way there is nothing I can do about it.

I[t's] going to be awfully hard for me to wait these next few days. The next week will seem like an eternity, honestly. But I'll just have to grin and bear it.

Adrienne and her boyfriend are going to be in N.Y. over the weekend. She said she won't stay at your hotel because she's afraid you might tell me tales. Evidently she doesn't trust herself, anyhow we don't trust her, not any of us.

We received cards today from Leon Nesbitt. It was nice of him to remember us. Please give him my regards if you see him in the meantime.

Luther, I'll write you the details of my trip later as I am not quite sure yet how I will come. I suppose though it will be by bus.

Thank you so very much for asking me and please write me soon.
Mary

Hotel Wellington
Seventh Avenue
Fifty-Fifth and Fifty-Sixth Streets
New York

Aug. 2, 1940
N.Y.C.

Dear Mary:

It is my regret that your vacation was thus arranged but I'll appreciate your one week.

How hard do you suppose it is with me to wait your arrival? I feel like I'm going to snap.

Listen, I don't care how you arrive—by plane or cow—just let me know which airport or cow pasture you're arriving at and so you get here on the 11th or before. Should you come by bus, come in at the 50th Street Station. Give me the correct time allowing for day light saving time.

Write the information immediately so I can make arrangements to meet you. If you can get in late Saturday night, that will be swell.

Please excuse this writing, but you understand.

"Luke"

The Letters

Wilkes-Barre, Pa
Aug. 7, 1940
Dear Luther,

Having received your letter I am all the more impatient. This week seems longer than even I could have imagined. What have you got that gets me?

This is just a note to let you know that I will arrive at 6:35 Standard time, 7:35 your time. Please don't get the hours mixed. I'd die.

Also I am coming by Greyhound since it's the only way I'm sure of and seeing as how a cow would be to slow, "Smarty."

Please try not to snap before I get there, I don't care what you do after as long as I'm there.
Mary

Wilkes-Barre, Pa
August 19, 1940
Dear Luther,

I'm keeping my promise and writing to you at the first opportunity I have. It goes without saying that I really enjoyed being with you. There is no better way in which I could have spent my vacation. Your company is all that I crave.

Already I am feeling quite lonely without you. But then that will make seeing you again so much more pleasure when you come.

Brother and Sister were quite elated with N.Y. They are already planning their next visit. I'm afraid you'll find the Brooks can be quite pestery. But I can't help it, they consider you one of the family, you see they've adopted you already. I hope you won't mind.

Sara was anxious to hear all about our visit and is planning a regular "Blitzkrieg" when she comes. She sends her regards to Fisher and wants you to thank him for all his kind regards.* You can tell him that I have related all to her that he asked me to.

It was so nice keeping up at night but I do hope you get rested up soon. Myself I don't mind being rather beat since being with you made me that way. I'm going to rest from now until your visit home whenever that will be. I want to be fresh and beautiful for your sake. You know they say sleep makes beauty. You'll know at least I tried.

Now please be a darling and answer very, very soon.

With all my love
Mary

*Mary was referring to Floyd Fisher, another of Luther's second cousins.

Hotel Wellington
Seventh Avenue
Fifty-Fifth and Fifty-Sixth Streets
New York

August 24, 1940
N.Y.C.

Dear Mary,

Your promptness in writing soon after your return was very much appreciated.

I'm very well pleased as to you enjoying your brief vacation here. As I have already told you—your happiness is my pleasure. I hope that soon we can enjoy each other's company without the returning home. Perhaps it [is] best that we stay away from each other a <u>short</u> while at the rate we were going anyway. It was so good and you were so sweet that I almost didn't care about anything else in the world. Our loneliness now will be compensated later.

It's really sweet to know that I am a part of a family that I have so much interest in. I hold a liking for each and every one of you, and a deep love for you (Skippy too.) You must inform them that I cannot accept their visit unless they stay a week or more, don't play me cheap. Tell Sara, Fisher is all aflutter and also someone else so be careful.*

I feel very guilty because I was so careless in looking up the timetable for "Gone with the Wind." I'm sure you were set on seeing it, in fact I was myself. Maybe it will still be down here when you return.

Johnny and Marjie apologize to each other for their misunderstanding Saturday night and all is well again. They insist that you have their address, also Champ, so here they are.

Mr. & Mrs. John Giles
287 Edgecomb Ave
Apt. 3C

Mr. & Mrs. Hayward Lambert
327 Edgecomb Ave.
Apt 4

That is very sweet of you to get plenty of rest to have more beauty, but you have enough for me. I suggest that you also had enough to drink for a while. Each time I've been with you I learn more about you and each time you become more interesting but I'm leery of you while drinking. Please be very careful while you drink. I'm not telling you this because I don't drink much but you'll agree with me that it is best after all.

All my friends thought you were very charming and they have considered with Emily in making your visit so pleasing.

Maybe some of the boys will be up for Labor Day—not certain yet.

Please let me hear from you soon. Let's write to each other more often.

Ever thinking of you

"Luke"

The Letters

August 30, 1940
Wilkes-Barre

Dear Luther,

It was nice as usual to hear from you. Your interest in my welfare is really most appreciated. I really deserved the scolding you gave me. You'll never know how very ashamed I am of myself. I must have completely forgotten my dignity. But please believe me, I do not make a habit of overindulging. For your sake I am trying to be a very good girl. I am truly sorry if in any way I embarrassed you and your friends.

I was very glad to hear that Marjorie and Johnny apologized and made up. But then I thought they would. Those little differences will recur between the most loving of couples, at least I'm told.

Sara and Sister want me to tell you that you needn't worry about their staying long enough. They usually have to be told to go.

I wish that the boys would have let us know whether or not they plan to come on Labor Day. Then we could plan something although everybody here is leaving for the week-end. Really, I never knew N.Y. to be so popular. Everybody and their brother intends to be there in the near future.

The baby parade has started. Alma Powell has a son, also the Lyle's. Johnny is the proudest father of all I'll ever see. I really envy them.

Luther, you can write me as often as you like. I never tire of reading your letters, you know that.

Think of me often and please remember me to your friends. My favorite song by the way is "Maybe.
Love
Mary

Hotel Wellington
Seventh Avenue
Fifty-Fifth and Fifty-Sixth Streets
New York

September 3, 1940
N.Y.C.

Dear Mary:

You will find this missive sort of long, please peruse it carefully. First in direct response to your letter, your being high was as not serious as you think it was. There wasn't any embarrassment and your dignity was the least bit alleviated, in fact you were quite amusing. Because of my interest in you I only mentioned it.

Still waiting for Lil and Sarah. Hope they didn't change their minds.

The proud mothers and fathers should be commended for their offspring. You know it must be quite a thrill to become a mother or a father.

For some time I've been confronted by my friends with marriage, why, I don't know. Now that they have seen and met you, the question seems to be put before me more tersely. Emily gave me a talking to the other day and when she got through my head was spinning like a top. Then Johnny and Margie put their bid in and I sorta felt pretty bad. While I thought very much about it, the reason for detaining I will explain later.

I guess I needed that push to wake me up. You know Mary, being away from you had its bad points and its good point. The bad point was my living alone made it hard to see another angle on life, but then the good point was that my being away served as a test to prove my love for you. A test I hope that you have had for me.

I feel that this marriage between we two is in need of mention now. I should be and am very grateful for you waiting as you did. Should I have received a letter telling me that you have found someone that you feel is more interested in you than I, I would have felt pretty bad, although I guess I deserved such. Furthermore, when you returned home last time I felt it more than ever. It was an indescribable feeling, like your best friend leaving you.

I am offering some plans and suggestions I want to confer with them and in return give me yours. First, as Emily and I see it, I wish you would ask your NY management to try and arrange that you be transferred down here. Just put the facts right to him. Tell him "my intended husband (you'll be speaking of me then—the buttons are justa poppin' off my shirt) is located and working in N.Y. Making it quite convenient if you would make that change since I feel that I can work with your company as long as possible." You know any old thing that you think will help you to stress your point.

I realize you have certain little obligations at home which I have also but they can be taken care of, should you live in N.Y. also. Now in the event that you cannot be transferred with the help of Emily and myself you have the privilege of staying here as long as you care to and look for work.

The reason for my detainment in asking you for your hand in marriage, as the old folks used to say, is I've been trying to establish myself to earn more money than I am now. Referring to the air conditioning and refrigeration course I am taking. I have about a hundred dollars in it and I still owe about a hundred and twenty-five. The time to finish the course and the time to finish paying for it will take another year. I am trying to avoid waiting until I finish to wed. In fact with your consent and if things seem within reason, I want to marry you soon after the first of nineteen forty-one. As I mentioned before, please give me your honest suggestion because you know this is something I really do not know anything about and I'll appreciate your help in the matter.

This is my true confession and not the kind you buy at the news stand.

We could make our home at Emily's until of course, things turn out better.

I suppose that is all I have to say except that Margie is writing to you some time. She really thinks you are very sweet.

Please answer and consider the facts soon.
"Luke"
P.S. I love you.

The Letters

Years after my father died, my mother confessed that she did not disclose the whole truth in this letter. "I didn't want to go to New York until we had a definite wedding date. I was afraid if I went sooner, your father might find an excuse to postpone getting married."

Wilkes-Barre, Pa
September 10, 1940
Dear Luther,

Your letter left me so breathless and overwhelmed that I'll never be quite the same.

It was so nice to hear of Emily and Margie and Johnny being interested in us. Tell them I appreciate the talking they've done.

Luther, really I don't know what to write about coming to N.Y. You see we have no store in N.Y. right now. For some reason or other it was discontinued. So that leaves the transfer business out, much to my regret.

It was sweet of Emily and you to give me the privilege of staying in N.Y. That would be quite all right if you could find something for me to do. I don't care what it is. Then meanwhile I could look for something better.

Otherwise Luther, I don't possibly see how I could manage to make the change. This is the only suggestion I can make right now.

It is so nice of you to want me to come to N.Y. to be with you. You know there is nothing I'd like better and I'll try very hard so that I might come.

I've talked your letter over with my mother and father and they leave everything up to me. So please help me to make the best of whatever we decide, won't you?

Tell Margie I'm waiting to hear from her and very soon.

I'm so glad you love me.

Mary

Hotel Wellington
Seventh Avenue
Fifty-Fifth and Fifty-Sixth Streets
New York

Sept. 16, 1940
N.Y.C.

Dear Mary:

I am very jubilant over the way you have received my humble offering. You are very sweet and it makes me all the more anxious to have you close to me. I've made several inquiries about work, also trying to stay in your line of work, but they tell me they'll let me know and others tell me your personal appearance would help very much more.

I still don't want to induce you to come unless you are perfectly willing because if you should become disgusted I would feel very much to blame. So I'll just continue to gather as much information as possible.

I am very grateful to your mother and father for their way of receiving the news of our intended union.

By the way our very sweet and amusing sisters are here. They are doing very nicely and still not over doing it. I've spent as much time with them as I possibly could and enjoyed it. They plan to return late Tuesday night or early Wednesday morning. I am going up to eat breakfast with them this morning. They'll have loads of things to talk about when they return so all of you have your ears sharpened up.

So again, I write that I am very anxious to see you here in N.Y. nearer to me. I feel that it is better for me and I'll try to make you like it. So keep your fingers crossed and I'll do likewise and perhaps fate will play one of his old tricks and bring us together soon I hope. We must try hard.

Listen for "Only Forever"

Oodles of Love

"Luke"

The Letters

Sept. 22, 1940
Dear Luther,

First I want to thank you for showing our "little" sisters such a wonderful week. They arrived home around two Wednesday morning and immediately I arose to hear all about it. I guess we talked for an hour and a half. We had so much to discuss. I must say Fisher did very well for himself while they were there.

More power to him. You are very kind to go to all the trouble of looking for work for me. I know it is no easy task and I do appreciate your every effort. I keep my fingers crossed constantly just in case.

We are rather excited here. Parran Foster's wife has a little girl and Evelyn Payne has a great big boy. Wilkes-Barre seems to be coming on like "Buster's gang." Heaven knows it can stand it, take it from me.

By the way I was asked to inform you why you always forget to ask about Lucy! She is really quite put out about it. She wants to know how you can think of me and forget her. It's really preposterous.

Now I must close. Sister and I are going calling this afternoon and she is waiting for me.

Please relay my regards to everyone.

My favorite this week is "Now I Lay Me Down to Dream," and I really do often.

Mary

Hotel Wellington
Seventh Avenue
Fifty-Fifth and Fifty-Sixth Streets
New York

September 30, 1940
N.Y.C.

Dear Mary:

I enjoyed seeing and being with your sisters. They are very sweet to have around. I'm sure Fisher enjoyed being in town with the Brooks. I'm sure you made his short [stay] worth his while. Sorry I couldn't accompany him as he asked me to. Give my thanks to Sara for her correspondences. Also tell her I will answer her letter soon. Thank you.

Memories of our being together last still linger with me. I wonder how long it will be before they are repeated, soon I hope. I grow quite lonesome for you any more, honest. I'm still trying to do all I can for you but I think you could do more for yourself, but of course I know how you feel about the matter. Nevertheless, you will always find me trying to help you in my humble way.

You must inform Lucy and all of your friends that your friends are definitely my friends. Although I do deviate much of my thoughts to you, tell her I must not lose my ranking with her. She is an Old Dear. Do you think that will console her?

Johnny and Margie are all excited because they have been assigned to one of the project houses. They are swell too. Tell more about it later.

The increase in our population is swell news. Tell them to keep the good work up. Keep sweet and my regards to the family.

"Luke"

The Letters

One day after this letter was written, Mary's Aunt Hattie passed away. Officially, the cause of death was chronic myocarditis and arteriosclerosis. My mother always said that she died of a 'broken spirit' following the death of her husband and the imprisonment of her son.

October 7, 1940
Wilkes-Barre
Dear Luther,

As I've written so many times it was to my utmost enjoyment to hear from you.

First, I want to tell you how much we really enjoyed having Fisher here with us. He came with the intention of leaving 3:15 Saturday morning, but he was just too reluctant to leave our Sara. He did manage to make the bus on Sunday at 3:15 A.M. We did have lots of fun though and we were very sorry to see him leave. For the past week we've received cards and more cards from all parts of the West. In fact Sara has a stack called the <u>Fisher Collection</u> dedicated to Floyd. This morning she received air mail from Monterey, California. Fast man that Fisher. Your mother came by to meet him on Sunday evening but she was a day too late. I was really sorry as she was disappointed.

I suppose you've heard about the big church conference etc., also of your friend Beville's having been ordained and receiving the West Pittston Church. I didn't know whether to congratulate him or offer him sympathy. After thinking it over I offered the former.

I do wish the "Gods" would be kind and set me right down in N.Y. with a job and everything my heart desires, which isn't so much considering. You see I also miss you very much and time does seem to go so slowly. It would be so nice really.

Please write me very soon and maybe I won't feel so blue.
Mary

Hotel Wellington
Seventh Avenue
Fifty-Fifth and Fifty-Sixth Streets
New York

October 16, 1940
N.Y.C.

Dear Mary:

Very much elated over your last letter. I've perused it several times only to enjoy it more each time.

You know I'm a subject to be selected for military service. I have just registered. So if I'm not called we will make definite plans for January. But if I am selected, well, plans will have to be altered and delayed so keep your fingers crossed.

I've been congratulated and asked about our marriage. I suppose you have also. Can't tell them much but I hope it comes true. It will.

Johnny and Margie have their own little apartment and they are very happy about it. I helped them move. What a task it was arranging the house when they both had different ideas, but it was fun.

Swell you enjoyed Fisher's company. I'm certain he enjoyed his short visit ten times as much. We also received cards from different points of the West. It's swell he reached his destination safe but I bet he would have been satisfied in Wilkes-Barre in the company of my very good friend Sara.

My sincere congratulations to my friend Beville on his achievement. May his followers be threefold.

Just in case you are interested the Bug's Formal is Wednesday November 13. Unless you kids come I will not attend this year.

Well nothing more except that I hope we can make some definite plans soon. My one desire is to have you here as soon as possible.

Incidentally, I also registered for the presidential election. You know it will be the first time I voted. I feel very important. I'm making myself a firm citizen of New York for us.

Well, expecting to hear from you soon

Love

Luke

P.S. For goodness sakes how is Lucy?

Wilkes-Barre
October 22, 1940
Dear Luther,

I enjoyed hearing from you. Like you I gave your letter several perusals for greater pleasure.

You can be sure I'll be keeping my fingers crossed against you being drafted for service. If that should happen my heart will break. I've so looked forward to being with you.

I appreciate very much you becoming a true citizen for both our sakes. We are also getting ready to vote. But then you know I'm an old hand at this since last year. Now Sara is being initiated, so you have something in common with each other.

I must tell you also that I've been congratulated and wished so much happiness that I should never be sad again. Everyone here wants to know our plans but I tell them to be patient, that I'll publish them for all the world to know when they are completed and I'll feel so proud, really I will.

Bill Grimes informed me that just to celebrate he's going to do his best to get high in honor of so great an occasion. I guess then he'll feel that he is really a man and he'll be paying us great homage.

Your mother came over the other day with a picture of a little boy in a leather jacket and asked me if I knew who it was. How could I have been mistaken so familiar a countenance? She was very proud of it and I don't blame her, you were very cute, believe me.

It was sweet of you to help Johnnie and Margie move into their new apartment. I'm positive with your help they have a very nice arrangement. Your such a handy person to have around the house (your mother told me so).

Write me too soon please
Love
Mary
P.S. Lucy sends her regards

Hotel Wellington
Seventh Avenue
Fifty-Fifth and Fifty-Sixth Streets
New York

October 29, 1940
N.Y.C.

Dear Mary:

Again I was pleased to read the writing of so sweet a person. Your writing spells all the symptoms of your charm.

Well you know time is getting shorter every day. We must not let anybody or anything disrupt our plans once they are made. I have been gathering some information as to the procedure one takes to enter into wedlock. Please find out from some reliable source in town as to whether you can obtain a license and be married all in one week. In N.Y. State you must wait two weeks to be married after obtaining a license. If up there it can be done in one week I will come up there if I can to do the honors. Of course do not rely on that too much because it is not certain yet. Perhaps you will have to come down here about two weeks before the date. I am contemplating on January 30th because that is my birthday. Receiving you as a present is supreme.

If you have any other plans please do not hesitate to mention them. After all you have as much privilege as I to make suggestions. Remember nothing is really definite yet but we will make plans to suit our convenience and means.

I was talking to Emily and she said she will make it light as possible for us and room is reserved for us. She may be home for Thanksgiving.

I appreciate those nice things my mother told you about me, after all mothers do that for their sons but I want to prove to you my worth. Those pictures, well you know they say all babies are cute so I was just an ordinary baby.

Like you I am asked questions and congratulated so often, gosh I didn't know so many people cared. Just tell them to keep their shirts on. Tell Bill Grimes I'll retaliate for him some day.

You know each time I write to you I have my radio on and the music gives out so if there seems to be rhythm in my letter you know the source it is derived. Right now the orchestra is playing "My Wonderful One." Quite appropriate I say.

Enclosed you will find a picture of Miss Rosalyn Lambert, offspring of Mr. and Mrs. Lambert. She is quite a miss. Also, the other youngsters that are my dear friends. They all express anxiety for your arriving here to socialize with them.

My regards to all and oodles of love to you.

"Luke"

Please answer soon.

Wilkes-Barre, Pa
November 4, 1940
Dear Luther,

    Just the pleasure of reading your letters adds so much to my life. I'll be forever indebted to you, believe me.

    It was awfully sweet of you to offer to come up here just to marry me. As far as I can gather, it takes about six days for a couple to marry. That includes the whole procedure, I believe. I'd love nothing better than being a birthday present to you. You make me feel very, very proud, Luther.

    Emily is awfully sweet to reserve her room for us. I'll wait until Thanksgiving to express all my appreciation. We['ll] certainly be looking for her then.

    Everyone here has been excited about the draft and the election. I shall spend a week rejoicing when it is all over. We were all wondering how you made out in the draft. Every one of us—family & friends included—kept our finger crossed for you as you suggested. I do hope it was to some avail.

    Fisher wrote Sara that he was entirely safe being somewhere in the 8,000's. It is too mixed up for me. I can't make head or tail out of all those numbers.

    Lucy and her friends are coming to N.Y. soon. They offered to bring me down Sunday if they can make the proper arrangements. I'll write you later concerning any plans as I am not quite sure if I can make it, but I will try to come.

    Remember me to your friends and please write me soon.
Love
Mary (My favorite song is "We Three")

Hotel Wellington
Seventh Avenue
Fifty-Fifth and Fifty-Sixth Streets
New York

Nov. 12, 1940
N.Y.C.

Dear Mary:

You really are a subject to the saying—"It's the little things that count so much," since you appreciate my humble letters. Thanks a thousand fold.

I wasn't quite so fortunate in the draft situation although I appreciate to the utmost you and family and friends who played so noble a part. My number was 2472 and it was drawn out of the fish bowl 1206th, therefore I'm supposed to be in the first draft. But don't let that worry you. I think I can get out of it. I have a little idea up my sleeve and it is legal too. I think it will work, nevertheless we will continue to make our plans for January 30-41.

Between the draft and my plan for us plus other matters I must face, I think I have aged ten years within the last two months but don't worry I have lots of affection in store for you. Now perhaps I cannot come up to marry you, if I can't I'll expect you down here about January 15th and you'll only need a one-way ticket. Everything is sorta topsy turvy so just hold tight.

Emily doesn't think she can come home now so don't depend on that. We are the most indefinite folks you have ever heard of, especially right at the present time.

Perhaps if you would have come down Sunday I wouldn't have let you go back anyway. Once I get you now there's no getting away. Did Lucy come? Charlie went to Rochester to see his mother and Wash. He sent us cards—having a swell time.

Nothing further but remember our date must not be changed.

My echo, my shadow and me send our love.

Listen for the Ink Spots version of "Your Breaking My Heart"

Love again

Luke

Wilkes-Barre, Pa

November 18, 1940

Dear Luther,

How can you say I appreciate only the little things in life? I consider you and your letters the biggest thing that ever happened to me. Please remember that.

Luther, I don't want you to worry about us. We can only hope for everything to work out for the best. If it should happen to be otherwise we'll just have to plan all over again and with better luck next time. I know you're doing your best for both of us and that is all you can do. Please stop worrying. I do want you to stay young for a long, long time. We have too much ahead of us.

We're sorry Emily won't be able to come for Thanksgiving. That reminds me, you're celebrating yours this week, are you not? I hope that all of you spend a most enjoyable day and I'm sure you will.

I was very sorry that we didn't get to N.Y. last Sunday. Lucy and her girl friend (another old maid) had one of their famous political arguments and no one went to N.Y. But since you harbor ulterior motives probably it was for the best. Although it is a lovely thought.

Do you know that I've never expressed my appreciation to you for telling us of the Bug's dance? But you understand how hard it is to get time off in the middle of the week. We thought about it often enough, though.

Also, Miss Roselyn Lambert's picture has made quite a hit in Wilkes-Barre. I can see where she will make a very popular debutante in the far future.

You can see by this letter that I have a slow one track mind but I get around to everything in time. Your song is colossal with me.

Loads and loads of love

Mary

The Letters

Hotel Wellington
Seventh Avenue
Fifty-Fifth and Fifty-Sixth Streets
New York

November 25th, 1940
N.Y.C.

Dear Mary,

    Your encouraging letter was easy to digest. If it were possible to love you any more I would but there isn't a bit of stray love to be found for you. At one time I use to scoff at the word love and the idea of marriage. Then at the first sight of you I began to feel somewhat of a change in my outlook of life only I was a little timid admitting it. And now I can't conceive anything but planning my life for you and with you. Since meeting I have derived so much pleasure at the sight of you, in your walk, in your talk, in your dress, the thrill of holding your hand and your caresses and your whole being in general. I even tingle at the mention of them. Please excuse this outburst of romantic literature but it's for you and far be it for me to hold out on you.

    I had a fairly nice Thanksgiving. I worked in the morning and the hotel served us a turkey dinner as usual. After coming home I dressed and went to call on Emily until about eight p.m. From there I want to see the Giles but Judy was out to my disappointment. From there I came home to listen to one of my favorite radio programs then I spent the rest of the evening at Lambert's playing cards and what not. That was my Thanksgiving Day program.

    So we will perform our ceremony down here. It will eliminate time and difficulty since you are coming anyway. So I can expect you here no later than the fifteenth of January. Before I forgot—bring your birth certificate in case there is some doubt about your age. If you have any

other plans or wishes please express them. I'm sure everything will be alright. I have lots of confidence in you and that alone helps us to begin. So I'll expect to hear from you soon.
Love
"Luke"

The Letters

December 2, 1940
Wilkes-Barre, Pa
Dear Luther,

You were very sweet to write me such a lovely letter. I've read it "umpteen" times enjoying it more each time. You've really made me terribly happy just by telling me how much you cared.

Your decision to be married in N.Y. suits me fine, although our families are quite disappointed. But we can make that up to them later in some way, I'm sure.

I'm just counting the days until January 15 just to see you. It seems an eternity since my vacation last summer and the time is really getting short.

Thank you for reminding me of my birth certificate. Really, I would have never thought of it. But then I didn't expect trouble about my age after I've been voting for two elections. But to be on the safe side I'll surely bring it.

We had a very quiet Thanksgiving visiting the Tylers in Scranton. Outside of a heavy snowfall it was the same as any other day. It was nice knowing you spent yours in such an enjoyable fashion. Your Thanksgiving greetings were received in the usual great big way by yours truly with my very most ultra appreciation.

Well Luther, be a good boy and write me real soon.

Anxious to hear from you

Love and more love

Mary

P.S. "I Give My Word" is my favorite right now, so listen to it for me please. Also excuse the writing but this pen is terrible.

Hotel Wellington
Seventh Avenue
Fifty-Fifth and Fifty-Sixth Streets
New York

December 9, 1940
N.Y.C.

Dear Mary:

Don't let your heart skip a beat or gasp for breath as Mrs. Lawrence did when she learned the information. I received my questionnaire and also I have been classified as 1A which is very dangerous but I received some further information and it is that should I be called it won't be until at least two months. Now you see within two months you will be Mrs. Snyder and the story will change. So in spite of it all you should not have anything to worry about. All I ask of you is to not make your date of arrival later than January 15th—if possible you may come two or three days before. After all it is too close for comfort. They boys are getting a big kick out of it all. They call me Captain Snyder and when I enter the locker room they say 'We're in the army now." They are a bunch of lugs though.

It's going to be lots of fun laughing, talking, listening to our favorite numbers and programs together not to mention the headaches and disappointments. Your personality and your charms exceed the wealth of any king. Let's get together. We have the symptoms of that same old story—of a boy and a girl in love.

Charles told me sometime ago that Louise was very serious but since then she has recovered nicely. Minnie and Rosabelle both went to see her.

Edgar and John were down sometime ago also. You know they always bring news when they come. Did you say you had a one track mind?

Should you have any clothes or what not you may send as much or as often as you wish either to Emily or myself. That will alleviate your luggage when traveling.

All the folks are waiting your arrival. Well nothing more at the present—waiting for your answer.

Love

"Luke"

Dec. 16, 1940
Wilkes-Barre, Pa
Dear Luther,

    I did more than gasp and lose a heart beat when I read your letter. How dare they do such a thing when we have already made so many plans. At least they had the decency to put it off for two months. But we'll truly have to hurry if we want to beat them. From what I hear over the radio and what I can gather from newspapers the situation is critical. Every time I read a paper or hear another report over the air my heart sinks ten feet. And I must confess after reading your letter I just about hit bottom. You are correct, everything is really getting to close for comfort. I'll be so terribly disappointed if in any way our plans are disrupted now. But I'm keeping my fingers crossed constantly for both our sakes.

    I received a letter from Louise just lately. She also told me that she had been very ill. Blood transfusions and oxygen tanks and all that goes with it. I was very sorry to hear that. Louise is a very sweet girl and I'm quite fond of her. We still miss her here in Wilkes-Barre. It was nice reading of her being better now.

    Well, Luther, I wish you the merriest of Christmas's. You're very sweet and I love you a lot.
Mary

Hotel Wellington
Seventh Avenue
Fifty-Fifth and Fifty-Sixth Streets
New York

Dec 23. 1940
N.Y.C.
Dear Mary:

More than happy to receive and read another of your encouraging letters.

Very much elated over your telegram of happiness. It in turn made me happy and also very proud to know that I am living to see you. Should the ring not be your size let it remain as is and when you arrive my jeweler will adjust to your finger size. Thank you, please.

Please convey my holiday greetings to Lucy, Adrienne and the others.

My mother was very pleased about her coat and she insists that I ask you about it. It's nice to know everyone is pleased—that is the way I like it to be.

I have nothing planned for Christmas—going to work part of the day—don't care anyway.

Please tell the family I'm the same old Luke with the same old thoughts for each and every one of them.

Much love
"Luke"

Although my mother got along well with her co-workers at Kempton's, and appreciated their wedding gifts, she told me late in her life that she actually resented the situation. "I was only paid five dollars a week, a lot less than the other girls, and by the time I left I was doing the same work. Plus, they made me wear a maid's uniform."

Wilkes-Barre, Pa
December 30, 1940
Dear Luther,

    I really meant to write sooner to ask if you enjoyed your Christmas etc. But I've been trying to recuperate from the rush. So help me may I never work through another such experience. Can you imagine seventy-five or more hours in one week? Really it's worse than a nightmare. It certainly takes the joy out of the rest of the holiday.

    Your ring was very lovely. It makes me feel so terribly proud to wear it. Everyone has complimented me on its beauty. I couldn't wait to go to work to show the girls. As usual I had to show the ring to Lucy first or her feelings would be hurt. She didn't believe me when I showed it to her. When she was finally convinced she had to shed tears of happiness for my sake. Poor Adrienne first put her head on my shoulder speechless. She couldn't think of a thing to say. She has been very sweet though, planning a shower for me before I leave, at her home. Only one sad thing, she has teased me to death about getting married. She tells all our regular customers that I'm a "peanut" bride-to-be. Sometimes I'm really awfully embarrassed and I do blush furiously, but I can't help it, she has no modesty whatever.

    Your mother was over the other night. She looked at my ring and said she was blinded, she was proud of you though, I could tell. She wants me to tell you that her coat is beautiful and I hope you'll like it because she did get it in my store. And we're proud of our merchandise.

Naomi Brown is visiting here. She told everyone that you had been called up for service. They come to me excitedly. I tell them what you have told me and pray that there has been no further developments. I was really quite upset at first, but I'm sure you'd have written me if there would have been anything further. At least I'm expecting you to do so immediately.

Oh, I must not forget or Sara will burst. Her Fisher sent the family a whole crate of oranges for Christmas. She wants you to know what a lot of "oomph" she has, you know a real "killer."

Well, Luther, I wish you a million joys in the New Year. Please stay sweet and write me very soon.

Love

Mary

P.S. I hope the robe fit. We measured it on Brother for a sort of idea of your size. I have no idea myself how men's sizes run.

Love again

Mary

Hotel Wellington
Seventh Avenue
Fifty-Fifth and Fifty-Sixth Streets
New York

January 3, 1941
N.Y.C.

Dear Mary:

So amused with your letter. Very happy to know you were pleased with the ring, the wedding ring matches it. The robe fit perfectly, Brother is a good model. I have it on right now. I am very proud of it. It's the first thing I mention if some asks me what I got for Christmas.

I'm sure you must have been very fatigued and worn out because of the holiday rush but when a store carries such merchandise expect such. After all my Mother buys only the best—for the least—I'm glad you both like her coat. I should be convinced.

I was <u>not</u> called for service yet and please get that straight. Of course I'd let you know if I were as much as I love and want you. I wouldn't trick you in coming here knowing that I was called. That is why I want you to come as soon as possible. We shall proceed to be married as soon as you arrive. Then we'll have the reception on the 30th. That is the plan that Emily and I have decided on. How is that with you?

As for the girls—Lucy, Adrienne and all the others, I'm sure you will miss them and tell them I'm grateful to each and every one for what ever they do for you.

All cards and what not were received and thank your Mother and Dad for their beautiful card. I shall keep it for ever. Also your "oomph" sister for her greetings. Won't I be especially proud to have so glamorous a sister-in-law. That was an extra-ordinary gift. I told all the fellows about it.

By the way also a thanks for your lovely card. I've got so much to thank you for so please don't hold it against me should I forget some little item.

I haven't any thing further to say until you arrive. So please let me know when you are arriving. I'll be very much pleased to see you—honest.

Lots of Love
"Luke"

Mary's last letter, which she dated incorrectly.

January 10, 1940

Wilkes-Barre, Penna.

Dear Luther,

This is just a little note to let you know that I will arrive in N.Y. at the Penn station at 12:15 on Monday afternoon. So please be sure to meet me. I think I've made the time, the place and the hour plain enough, I mean so you will have no trouble locating me.

Looking forward to seeing you.

Mary

Mary and Luke

My parents were married in St. Mark's United Methodist Church, on January 30, 1941, my father's thirtieth birthday. Dr. Samuel Sweeney, Pastor, performed the ceremony. The official witnesses were Thomas Busch, cousin Emily's husband, and Hayward Lambert, Luther's close friend he called Champ. Neither Maud nor Mary's family were present. Following the ceremony, Emily and Thomas hosted a small reception in an empty apartment in 409 Edgecombe Avenue, the building they managed.

Most of my father's friends called him Luke, not Luther. After they married, my mother also began to call him Luke.

Within a short time after the wedding, my mother became pregnant. Knowing they couldn't stay with Emily and her husband once the baby arrived, my father began looking for a better opportunity than his job at the hotel. Lydia James, my mother's cousin whose mother Irene drowned in 1895, had half-brothers and sisters in New Haven, Connecticut. Through Lydia, my parents learned that Winchester Repeating Arms, a gun manufacturer in New Haven, was hiring workers for round-the-clock shifts to make guns for the war effort. Hundreds of African Americans, mostly from the south, poured into New Haven to work there. In June of 1941, my parents hitched a ride to New Haven with one of Lydia's relatives and with little more than hope of my father finding work.

New Haven, home to Yale University, is a small coastal city with a beautiful harbor. African Americans had lived in New Haven almost since its founding by Puritans in 1635. The 1790 census recorded two hundred and five Blacks. By 1820, the number of Blacks had risen to six hundred and twenty-two. Although there were anti-slavery advocates in New Haven, most Black citizens faced crushing racial oppression. They were limited to certain occupations and restricted to living in segregated areas.

In the 1940s, New Haven was still segregated and opportunities were limited. Luckily, due to the need for workers, my father was quickly hired at Winchesters. Finding housing was a bigger challenge. The neighborhoods open to African Americans were overflowing with newcomers and apartment rents were skyrocketing beyond my parents reach. For the first few months, all they could afford was a room in a boarding house.

Shortly after my parents arrived, her brother Clarence quickly followed to also find work. He shared the same rented room with my parents. My father and mother sought better housing, but were turned away everywhere they went to rent a suitable apartment. Hearing how my parents and uncle were living—three to a bed, with a baby on the way—my grandparents came to New Haven to help, bringing along Sara and Lillian. Stella went alone in search of a place to live. She found an apartment in a two-family house in the Italian section of the Hill neighborhood where the whole family could stay in relative comfort.

In the fall of 1941, Sara met Julius Arthur Dixon, a local man who was working as a waiter at the time. After just a six-week courtship, they were married on November 6, 1941. Soon their first baby was on the way.

My brother Roy Brooks Snyder was born December 2, 1941. My mother was still in the hospital on December 7th when Pearl Harbor was attacked. Everyone knew that meant the United States would enter the war.

Sara's son William David Dixon was born on August 26, 1942. Stella and Gus were overjoyed to have two grandsons, but the family's jubilation was cut short. My grandfather Clarence had found work at the Harlem Barber Shop in New Haven. Around mid-October, he fell ill and was hospitalized. A month later on November 21, he passed away from miliary tuberculosis, an acute form of the disease. He was sixty-three. My mother and father took his remains back to Catawissa on the train, so that he could be laid to rest next to his sister Sara Jane in the Greenwood Cemetery.

Needless to say, my grandfather's death was a devastating loss. As reflected in the letters, my grandfather was the adored head of his family. My grandmother was left a young widow whose own health was always a concern due to her chronic asthma. My father became the one my grandmother, my mother, and her siblings leaned on for support.

In February 12, 1943, my mother's brother Clarence enlisted in the army. Because of his light skin and straight hair, the Army recruiting officers did not believe he was Black. The officers thought he was claiming to be Black so that he would not be sent into combat, since at the time Black troops only served in noncombat roles. He eventually convinced them of the truth and spent much of his military service in Southeast Asia. He did not return to New Haven until 1946.

My grandmother Stella, just forty-six, perhaps fearful of being on her own for the first time in her life, remarried on August 14, 1943. My mother and her siblings were shocked and angry, feeling her remarriage was too soon. Her new husband was also an African American named Samuel George Gardner, fifty-seven, a native of Hampton, Virginia.

He was a machine operator who owned a small house at 566 Orchard Street. Stella was his third wife.

Shortly after the marriage, my brother Dale William was born on August 24, four weeks premature, tiny but healthy enough to be brought home. A few days after, my mother's youngest sister Lillian eloped to Maryland with her boyfriend from Wilkes-Barre, Harry Paul Brown. On September 5, Sara's second child, Barbara Ann, was born.

In the fall of 1944, Maude suffered a stroke. Fortunately, she had visited New Haven in 1942 to see her first grandson Roy. After lingering for months without regaining consciousness, she died on February 13, 1945, taking the secret of the name of my father's father with her to the grave. I identify with anyone who doesn't have a relationship with their father—not knowing the name of our paternal grandfather was always gap for me and my siblings. I feel connected to Maude, since I have also remained unmarried (but childless). From my father's letters, she comes across as a doting mother and a beloved member of her family. I wish she had laid aside her own feelings of guilt and shame to tell my father the truth about his father.

Maude's death only added to my family's already unbearable grief. A month before Maude's death, my grandmother Stella suffered an unusually severe asthma attack on the afternoon of January 18, 1945. My father drove her to a doctor who gave her a shot of epinephrine. In the car returning home, Stella suffered a heart attack and died in my father's arms before he could reach the hospital. She was only forty-eight. Clarence would not learn of his mother's death until he returned from the war. Needless to say, her daughters were inconsolable.

Stella or Gus were two daring souls who defied society to live the life they wanted. At the same time, they were just an ordinary married couple raising a family. Gus was the breadwinner and stalwart head of his family. He was the disciplinarian who would use the strap when his four rowdy children were out of control. The way he dropped everything to be near his children in New Haven when they needed him, reflects the enormity of his love for them.

Stella was a tireless and creative homemaker. She made her children's clothes, canned fruits and vegetables, and wasn't squeamish about wringing the neck of a live chicken to cook for dinner. With all she had to do, she would hand-paint cards at Christmas time to earn a few extra dollars so she could afford gifts for her children.

Sadly for me, Maude, Stella and Gus all died before I was born. When I was a small child, I asked my mother if they would know me when I reached heaven. She assured me they would greet me with open arms.

My parents and brother Roy.

My father and grandmother Maude holding Roy, summer 1942.

My maternal grandfather, Clarence Augustus Brooks II.

My maternal grandmother, Stella May Paul Brooks Gardner.

Lillian holding nephew Roy, and Sara holding her son William (Billy). Circa 1942.

Clarence holding nephew Roy, spring 1942.

Roy with his little brother Dale, summer 1944.

Mary and Luke

After the war years, work at Winchester slowed and my father was laid off. He tried operating his own business: Snyder Trucking. He hauled everything from trash, to furniture, to merchandise for anyone willing to hire him. The business rarely provided an adequate income due to the cost of maintaining the truck, and the only artifact remaining is a single pencil I keep in a vase.

Following the demise of his business, my father worked for several years as the produce manager for a local grocery store, Schiffrin's Market on Dixwell Avenue, in the heart of one of New Haven's African American neighborhoods. He later worked as a superintendent for a local realtor who owned several properties, and eventually landed a job at Yale University as the foreman for the internal mail team. When my brother Roy was admitted to the University of Connecticut in 1959, he worked week-ends as a bartender for a caterer to pay for Roy's education.

My father was diagnosed with prostate cancer in 1969. For the next four years, he suffered through many surgeries and painful treatments, accepting whatever experimental procedures the Yale physicians proposed to try and stay alive.

Despite her sometimes feisty temper, despite the financial stresses, and the ups and downs of family life, my father loved my mother to his last breath. His dying command for me and my brothers was, "Take care of your mother." Near the end, he tenderly held my mother's hand in his and whispered, "Mary, you have been a blessing and a joy to me." He died just after midnight on April 2, 1973 with my mother and Roy at his side. His funeral was held a few days later at St. Luke's Episcopal Church where we worshipped, and where he served as an usher and member of the Men's Club.

To console herself, my mother reread the letters again and again. The person revealed in my father's love letters is not the man I remember. Around the house my father was a quiet man who loved listening to jazz, loyally followed his favorite baseball team the (Dodgers until they abandoned Brooklyn, then the Mets) and the Giants during football season. His open expressions of love and affection were a surprise to read. I do know my father was a gentleman in every sense of the word. He never cursed in front of me or my mother; he only drank an occasional beer, and he never laid a hand on me. My mother told me that once she asked him to spank me when I was especially unruly and he refused saying, "I never hit a woman in my life. I'm not going to start with my own daughter."

I was a sophomore in college when my father died, but his humble wisdom shaped my career. When I was a sophomore in high school, my father insisted I sign up for a typing course even though I was on the college track and that was part of the business curriculum. It was 1967 and I argued that I was not going to be a secretary. His reasoning: it was a skill that I would find useful even if I wasn't a secretary. He insisted and I caved. Later, when I was still early in my career, the desktop computer was introduced in my company. While my male counterparts hunted and pecked their way around the keyboard, I worked rings around them, earning three promotions in quick succession. Dad, you were right!

The second bit of wisdom was imparted in the car as he was driving me to my first real job (other than babysitting). I was to bus tables in a dining hall in Yale University. I was sixteen and remember sitting next to him in our ten-year-old old black Mercury as he drove me to Yale for my first day of work. "Now, Jill" he started, there's only two things you need to do to keep a job; do what you're told and be on time."

Over the years, I have reflected on the challenge of that message. I've witnessed so many people lose a job because they couldn't deliver a project on time, or simply arrive to work on time. I've also observed many workers who had a difficult time accepting that their boss had the right to tell them what to do and when to do it. I know I would not be who I am today without the love and guidance of my dad. He (quite deliberately I know now) taught me three things my mother never learned to do: to swim, to ride a bike and to drive. He planted the idea in me very early that I was to go to college. When I was very small, he read Aesop's fables to me and taught me several French words and phrases. Though only a high school graduate, he remembered enough of his high school algebra to help me with my homework. Forty years after his own high school graduation, he could still recite Polonius's speech to his son from *Hamlet* in its entirety. It only occurred to me recently that he must have been on a college preparatory track in high school, but was unable to attend himself, so he fulfilled his dream through his children. I'll never forget how proud he was the first day he drove me to college.

Unfortunately, I was only nineteen when he died, and in some ways our relationship hadn't healed from my challenging teenage years. One painful incident caused a deep rift in our relationship when I was a senior in high school. It was all about my hair. I wanted to wear a natural (we called it an Afro back then). He absolutely hated it. I had my high school graduation picture taken with my 'fro and he refused to have it displayed in the living room. I had my high school picture retaken with my hair straightened but the incident left me feeling conflicted and wounded. I did not attend my college graduation—I couldn't bear the thought that my beloved father wouldn't be there to see it. At the same time, I remained resentful over the incident for many years.

I understand now that my father grew up in different times and that many in his generation were ashamed of Black hair. Reading his letters has been very healing and helped me to finally let go of those negative feelings.

I was born in 1953 with a severe clubfoot. Clubfoot describes an abnormality in which a baby's foot is twisted out of position. The term clubfoot refers to the way the foot is positioned at a sharp angle to the ankle, like the head of a golf club. Clubfoot can be mild or severe, affecting one or both feet. The foot may be turned so severely that it actually looks as if it's upside-down. This is how my right foot appeared at birth.

Clubfoot is the most common crippling deformity in the developing world, affecting approximately one-hundred and fifty thousand infants each year. There are high incidences of untreated clubfoot and the untreated deformity leaves the individual unable to walk without great pain and unable to carry out daily tasks. To be clear, this often means a desperate life of street-begging.

Both my father and my mother dedicated themselves to ensuring I had the treatment I needed to walk normally. We had access to specialists at Yale University, who knew what to do to correct my clubfoot, but it took twelve years of casts, braces, crutches, and special shoes. My mother tirelessly took me for countless doctor visits and fittings, riding the bus and sometimes walking long distances. My father would massage my ankle every night to relieve the pain and stiffness. I am deeply thankful to them for their care.

I have happy childhood memories of many summer Sundays at the beach. My father and my Uncle Harry would head to Connecticut's Hammonasset State Park early in the morning "to get a spot," and set up the grills, tables, and umbrellas. The rest of the clan—my mother, Sara, Lillian, and Clarence and their spouses and children would trail about an hour or two later. By then, Uncle Harry would have sausages and home fries cooking on one grill, with coffee percolating on another. It always smelled so good! We would spend the day playing in the ocean, walking along the water's edge, and of course, eating hot dogs and burgers, fried chicken and potato salad.

Roy, Jill, and Dale. Circa 1955.

My parents were devoted to their children's development. In the 1950's, Mary was an original member of the New Haven Chapter of Jack & Jill of America, a national organization for African American mothers founded to provide social, cultural and educational activities for children.

Both Mary and Luke approached their role of preparing us for adulthood seriously. They were strict about manners and took us to church. They saw themselves as our primary educators and filled our home with books, exposing us to literature early so that we would love reading. They took advantage of the arts available in New Haven because of Yale University. We attended symphony concerts at Yale's Woolsey Hall and plays at the Yale Repertory Theater. The first theater production I saw was *Julius Caesar* and I was instantly a lover of Shakespeare.

Acutely aware of the world we were entering, they also prepared us to cope with racism and bigotry. In 1959, when I was in kindergarten,

I made friends with a little white girl named Caroline. One day she invited me to her home to play after school. My parents agreed that I could spend an hour and then my father would pick me up. When Caroline and I arrived at her home, her mother took one look at me and said, "You can't come in here," slamming the door in my face. I left in tears, and when I reached home my surprised mother asked me what happened. She immediately understood. "Jill," she said with her arm around me, "there are people who won't like you because you're colored. But always remember, it's not about you, it's about them. There is something wrong with their minds and they take it out on other people." Then she added, "But never let racism be an excuse for not doing your best." The next day she took me to the library and picked out several books for me to read on African American heroes like Harriet Tubman, Booker T. Washington, Mary McLeod Bethune, and George Washington Carver.

Our family's resolve in the face of racism was tested in the mid-1960s when we moved from New Haven to West Haven, an adjacent suburb. Our new white neighbors weren't happy there were Black people moving into their neighborhood. We woke up one morning with *Niggers* scrawled in big letters across the front of our house. My mother and father decided not to do anything about it. My defiant mother exclaimed, "Let them see what kind of people live here!" The ugly graffiti remained there for almost a year. Our home became an attraction. People came from all over to see it. Finally, after months of silence, several neighbors apologized. One morning we woke to find the epithet had been painted over during the night.

Mary was a wonderful homemaker and an excellent cook, especially expert in the German and British recipes passed down through her mother's side of the family. My favorites were shepherd's pie, pork and sauerkraut, shoo-fly pie, blanc mange, and Yorkshire pudding. She didn't work a full-time job until 1969, when my father was diagnosed with cancer. Realizing that she would need to have her own income, she took a position at local insurance company microfilming claims. In the late 1970s, she was hired as a research assistant in Yale's Wright Nuclear Structure Laboratory, supporting Robert Steiner, a doctoral candidate in advanced nuclear research. She was trained to scan images from the nuclear accelerator and record traces of a specific type of nuclear particle.

Her direct supervisor was Professor Horace Dwight Taft, a grandson of President William Howard Taft. She worked for him until he suddenly died from of a heart attack on February 12, 1983 while working in his office. My mother saved many of his short notes to her which he always signed 'H. Taft.'

My mother often told me that she wrote messages on a computer to other researchers at MIT and the University of Chicago. It wasn't until years later that I realized she was one of the early users of the Internet. Because of her support, Dr. Steiner presented my mother a copy of his Ph.D. thesis. He inscribed a personal message, saying, "For Mary, I couldn't have done it without you! With deep gratitude and lasting friendship, Rob."

Even though my mother worked after my father died, her income was not sufficient to sustain her. My brothers and I took care of her, providing her a home. For many years she and I lived together. Her health declined due to a heart condition, and with unbelievable courage and a deep religious faith, she survived three separate open-heart surgeries. Sadly, the oxygen deprivation to her brain while being connected to the heart-lung machines led to slowly advancing dementia. Despite this, she grittily continued to work when she could, and retired from Yale in 1985.

After retiring, she began painting as a hobby to fill her time and it wasn't until reading my parents' letters that I learned being an artist was a long suppressed dream. Her simple but tender paintings are my most prized possessions.

My mother spent nearly three and one-half years in the memory section of the Miami Jewish Home for the Aged. She never knew that my brother Dale had predeceased her. He had retired to Miami Beach, Florida, after being a Yale policeman for twenty-six years. He died suddenly on December 1, 2004, of a heart attack, leaving me, his two sons, Darryl and Sean, my brother Roy, and Roy's wife, Iris, bereft and inconsolable.

My mother died peacefully on September 1, 2007. Several months before her death, on a day when she was more lucid than usual, I asked her if she remembered her husband Luke. A long pause ensued while she gazed into the distant past. "I was married?" she asked. "Yes, Mom," I replied, "You were married to Luther William Snyder for thirty-two years. He was the father of your children—me and Roy and Dale." Another long pause. "Oh, yeah. I remember him. He was a very nice man."

I recently found a prayer my mother wrote that she dated June 1974. It was tucked in a box with condolence cards we received when

Mary and Luke

my father died the year before. It's written in the old Episcopal prayer book style.

> *Praise be to God for giving me the blessing of having been loved and having loved so wonderful a person as my husband Luther. I thank Thee, dear Father, for this greatest of all blessings. Also for my three wonderful children, with which we were blessed, I truly give thanks. Amen.*

> Dear Father,
> May he enjoy eternal life in Thy Presence, in Thy Peace and in Thy Love. And may we be joined in that bright future for all eternity. Amen.
> Mary

Christmas 1969: Mary, Dale, Luther, Roy, Jill

Epilogue

My great-grandfather, Charles Paul, died in July 1953 after a long illness. When my grandfather Gus died, Charles told people in Catawissa that he regretted how he had treated Gus and that Gus had turned out to be his best son-in-law. Charles sent a message to my mother and her siblings, asking to meet with them. They refused.

Mary Paul died in February 1956 at the age of eighty of a heart attack. Her obituary says that she was survived by three daughters, two sons and several grandchildren and great-grandchildren. There is no mention of Stella.

After returning from the war, my Uncle Clarence married Osceola Cullen, a distant cousin of poet Countee Cullen. They had two daughters, Phyllis and Cheryl. Uncle Clarence had a wonderful sense of humor, mostly poking fun at himself, not others. He seemed to be always laughing, but before he died from cancer in 2005, I asked him if he remembered his childhood in Bloomsburg. Choking back tears, He simply replied, "It was hard—really, really hard."

My dear Aunt Sara died in 2011. She had become a devout Jehovah's Witness, but never lost the wry sense of humor displayed in the letters. I have many wonderful memories of family picnics in her backyard, spending long hours playing croquet, volleyball, and card games. In addition to my cousins William David (Bill) and Barbara Ann, she had two other children: Robert Henry (Hank) and Karen Irene. She enjoyed

Epilogue

her later years living in an apartment attached to the home of Barbara and her husband, Nathan Qualls, and spending time with her children and fourteen grandchildren.

My mother's youngest sister Lillian, who her nieces and nephews affectionately call Aunt Sissy, is still living and resides with her daughter Sharon and grandson Aaron on Long Island. Aunt Sissy was a fashionable career woman who was a mentor and role model for me. She still inspires me.

Her beloved husband of sixty-two years, Harry, also died in 2011. Uncle Harry was the favorite uncle of many of his nieces and nephews. Whenever we needed help, we could show up at his door and he would take us in and help us solve our problems.

Harry was seriously wounded in World War II. A few years before his death he opened up to me for the first time, describing how he was injured:

> "I was in an all-Black unit on Okinawa. During the day, we would repair the runways after the Japanese bombed them at night. After we repaired the runways, our pilots would make bombing runs during the day. Then the Japanese figured out what was going on, and bombed the runways one day while we were working. I don't remember feeling anything, but all of a sudden I started bleeding from every opening."

Harry had severe concussion injuries and spent months in the hospital recovering.

After her father's death, my mother never saw any of her Parks relatives again. She didn't know that John Frank Parks Jr. served most of his prison sentence for killing his father and was released in the early 1950s. Following his imprisonment, he worked at Magee Carpet

Company and later the Magee Transportation Museum. He passed away in 1978.

It was while reading the newspaper articles about the Parks murder that I found a clue about the fate of his sister Helen, who had graduated from Bloomsburg College and taught at Tuskegee. A reporter covering the Parks story for the Bloomsburg *Morning Press* wrote a detailed description of the Parks family living room including the following:

> "The first floor parlor is filled with pictures of the family, including one of a family group of Parks' late daughter Helen and her family. She taught for a number of years at Tuskegee Institute, Alabama, the institution for the education of Negroes founded by Booker T. Washington. Helen later married a professor at the college."

My mother knew that Helen had moved south after college to teach but in her later years couldn't recall which institution. Even when dementia had begun to take its toll, she often wondered aloud why she had never heard anything of Helen since her own childhood. She was never told that Helen had died in the 1930's.

Helen had married Conrad Hutchinson who also worked at Tuskegee. Their son, Conrad Hutchinson Jr., became a musician. In the 1960s, he was the highly regarded and innovative leader of the Grambling State University marching band. I only learned this recently after connecting with my cousin Camille Shootes, one of Helen's grandchildren.

On my father's side of the family, his cousin David Haley, who had been hospitalized for severe emotional issues following his young wife's death from tuberculosis, was never released from the Retreat Mental Hospital in Pennsylvania. He wrote many letters to Emily asking her

Epilogue

to sign for his release. Emily always refused, fearful that David would take his son, her beloved Sonny, away from her. From time to time, my parents would discuss David's sad plight and briefly consider if they could accept responsibility for him. Shamefully, he was abandoned by everyone, and David died in the Retreat Hospital in the 1960s.

As an adult, Sonny became an alcoholic. He married a woman from Bermuda and died there in the early 1970's from kidney disease.

Sources

Battle, J.H. "Catawissa Township; this portion of The History of Columbia and Montour Counties, Pennsylvania." Made possible through the efforts of transcriber: Cindy Saniter. Accessed January 1, 2015, www.pagenweb.org/~columbia/catawid.htm

"Brud Holland," The National Football Foundation and College Hall of Fame, Inc., accessed January 1, 2015, www.Footballfoundation.org.

Charles L. Blockson. *African Americans in Pennsylvania: A History and Guide.* Baltimore: Black Classic Press, 1994

Dobbins, *Oxford Online, The New Grove Dictionary of Jazz, 2nd edition,* Oxford University Press: 2007-2013

Gray, Christopher. "Streetscapes: 409 Edgecombe, An Address That Drew the City's Black Elite." The New York Times Company, July 24, 1994. Accessed Dec. 31, 2014, www. NY Times.com/7/24/1994/realestate/streetscapes/409 Edgecombe Ave.

Gray, John. *Venus and Mars on a Date: A Guide for Navigating the 5 Stages of Dating to Create a Loving and Lasting Relationship.* New York: HarperPerennial: A Division of Harper Collins Publishers, 1999

Sources

Francis, Thomas. "Tommy Dorsey." *Oxford Online, The New Grove Dictionary of Jazz, 2nd edition*, Oxford University Press: 2007-2013

Hoover, Brett. "Celebrating Black History Month: Profiles from the Ivy League's Black History-Ben Johnson." 1 Jan 2009. Accessed Dec. 31, 2014, www.Ivy50.com.

Hosiasson, José. "Cab Calloway." *Oxford Online, The New Grove Dictionary of Jazz, 2nd edition,* Oxford University Press 2007-2013

Kaas, L. Michael, "History of the Pennsylvania Anthracite Region" (presented at the 16th Annual Conference, Lackawanna Heritage Valley Center, Scranton, Pennsylvania, June 16-20 2005). Mining History Association, accessed January. 1, 2015, www.mininghistoryassociation.org/scrantonHistory.htm.

Kenselaar, Robert. "Don Redman," *Oxford Online, The New Grove Dictionary of Jazz, 2nd edition*, Oxford University Press: 2007-2013.

Koslow, Phillip, editor. *New York Public Library African American Desk Reference*; New York: A Stonesong Press Book; John Wiley & sons, Inc., 1999

"Liberty The American Revolution: Chronicle of the Revolution-Hessians," *Public Broadcasting Service.* Accessed January 1, 2015, www.pbs.org/ktca/liberty/popup_hessians.html

Lynch, Hollis."African American life during the Great Depression and the New Deal." Encyclopedia Britannica, Inc., September 9, 2014. Accessed. January 1, 2015, http://www.britannica.com/blackhistory/article-285193

Magda, Matthew S. *"The Welsh in Pennsylvania, The Peoples of Pennsylvania Pamphlet No. 1."* Pennsylvania Historical & Museum Commission, Commonwealth of Pennsylvania, 1998. Accessed January 3, 2015, www.portal.state.pa.us/portal/server.pt/community/groups/4286/welsh/471948

"Medical Use of Cocaine." American Academy of Otolaryngology: Head and Neck Surgery, Last revised May 6, 2013. Accessed January 3, 2015. http://www.entnet.org/Practice/policyMedicalUseCocaine.cfm

Moss, Emerson I., *African Americans in the Wyoming Valley: 1778-1990*; Wilkes-Barre, Pa: Wyoming Historical and Geological Society and the Wilkes University Press, 1992

Platt, Orville H., "Negro Governors in *Papers of the New Haven Colony Historical Society*", Vol VI, 1900, pp. 333-334

Robinson, J. Bradford, "Ella Fitzgerald", *Oxford Online, The New Grove Dictionary of Jazz, 2nd edition*, Oxford University Press 2007-2013

Remini, Robert V. *A Short History of the United States.* New York:Harper Perennial; Harper Collins Publishers. 2008

Robinson, J. Bradford and Kernfeld, Barry, "Jimmy Lunceford", *Oxford Online, The New Grove Dictionary of Jazz, 2nd edition*, Oxford University Press: 2007-2013

Robinson, J. Bradford, "William 'Count' Basie", *Oxford Online, The New Grove Dictionary of Jazz, 2nd edition*, Oxford University Press: 2007-2013

Sources

Swanson, Catherine. "Dressing up Like a Crusader: Knights of the Golden Eagle." Scottish Rite Museum and Library, posted Sept. 21,. 2010. Accessed January 1, 2015, www.nationalheritagemuseum.typepad.com/library_and_archives/knights-of-the-golden-eagle/

"The Quaker Province 1681-1776." Pennsylvania Historical & Museum Commission, Commonwealth of Pennsylvania. Accessed Dec. 31, 2014. www.portal.state.pa.us/portal/server.pt/community/overview_of_pennsylvania_history/4281/1681-1776__the_quaker_province/478727

"This day in History, September 16: United States Imposes a Draft." A&E Television Networks, LLC, Accessed January 1, 2015, www.history.com/this-day-in-history/united-states-imposes-the-draft.

Warner, Robert Austin. *New Haven Negroes: A Social History.* New Haven: Yale University Press, 1940

*The reader will notice most of the public websites have a December 2014 or January 2015 access date. Although I completed most of the research between 2010 and 2013, I neglected to note the access dates for the web pages I found. Therefore, I re-accessed most pages as I was finalizing the book for publication.

Census citations

All census information was obtained from Ancestry.com and The Church of Jesus Christ of Latter-day Saints.

Rudy	Andruz	1910 U.S. Federal Census [database on-line]. Provo, UT, USA: Ancestry.com Operations, Inc.,2006
Daniel	Britton	1860 U.S. Federal Census [database on-line]. Provo, UT, USA: Ancestry.com Operations, Inc.,2009
Daniel	Britton	1870 U.S. Federal Census [database on-line]. Provo, UT, USA: Ancestry.com Operations, Inc.,2009
Daniel	Britton	U.S. City Directory, 1821-1989 (Beta) [database on-line]. Provo, UT, USA: Ancestry.com Operations Inc. 2011
Mary	Britton	1870 U.S. Federal Census [database on-line]. Provo, UT, USA: Ancestry.com Operations, Inc.,2009
Clarence A	Brooks	1930 U.S. Federal Census [database on-line]. Provo, UT, USA: Ancestry.com Operations, Inc.,2002
Clarence Augustus	Brooks	1910 U.S. Federal Census [database on-line]. Provo, UT, USA: Ancestry.com Operations, Inc.,2006
William	Davies	1910 U.S. Federal Census [database on-line]. Provo, UT, USA: Ancestry.com Operations, Inc.,2006

Census citations

Louise	Downey	1930 U.S. Federal Census [database on-line]. Provo, UT, USA: Ancestry.com Operations, Inc.,2002
Washington	Downey	1920 U.S. Federal Census [database on-line]. Provo, UT, USA: Ancestry.com Operations, Inc.,2010
Joshua	Enty	1860 U.S. Federal Census [database on-line]. Provo, UT, USA: Ancestry.com Operations, Inc.,2009
Elmer	Fisher	1900 U.S. Federal Census [database on-line]. Provo, UT, USA: Ancestry.com Operations, Inc.,2004
Elmer	Fisher	1910 U.S. Federal Census [database on-line]. Provo, UT, USA: Ancestry.com Operations, Inc.,2006
Elmer	Fisher	1920 U.S. Federal Census [database on-line]. Provo, UT, USA: Ancestry.com Operations, Inc.,2010
Elmer	Fisher	1930 U.S. Federal Census [database on-line]. Provo, UT, USA: Ancestry.com Operations, Inc.,2002
Harriet	Fisher	1880 U.S. Federal Census [database on-line]. Provo, UT, USA: Ancestry.com Operations, Inc.,2010
John	Foster	1930 U.S. Federal Census [database on-line]. Provo, UT, USA: Ancestry.com Operations, Inc.,2002
David	Haley	1940 U.S. Federal Census [database on-line]. Provo, UT, USA: Ancestry.com Operations, Inc.,2012
Delaphine	Haley	1920 U.S. Federal Census [database on-line]. Provo, UT, USA: Ancestry.com Operations, Inc.,2010
Delaphine	Haley	U.S. City Directory, 1821-1989 (Beta) [database on-line]. Provo, UT, USA: Ancestry.com Operations Inc. 2011

Beville	Highsmith	1940 U.S. Federal Census [database on-line]. Provo, UT, USA: Ancestry.com Operations, Inc.,2012
Christopher	Hillman	1930 U.S. Federal Census [database on-line]. Provo, UT, USA: Ancestry.com Operations, Inc.,2002
H	Jones	1860 U.S. Federal Census [database on-line]. Provo, UT, USA: Ancestry.com Operations, Inc.,2009
Henry	Jones	1850 U.S. Federal Census [database on-line]. Provo, UT, USA: Ancestry.com Operations, Inc.,2009
Henry	Jones	1870 U.S. Federal Census [database on-line]. Provo, UT, USA: Ancestry.com Operations, Inc.,2009
Henry	Jones	1880 U.S. Federal Census [database on-line]. Provo, UT, USA: Ancestry.com Operations, Inc.,2010
Charles A	Paul	1900 U.S. Federal Census [database on-line]. Provo, UT, USA: Ancestry.com Operations, Inc.,2004
Charles A	Paul	1910 U.S. Federal Census [database on-line]. Provo, UT, USA: Ancestry.com Operations, Inc.,2006
Charles A	Paul	1930 U.S. Federal Census [database on-line]. Provo, UT, USA: Ancestry.com Operations, Inc.,2006
James	Paul	1910 U.S. Federal Census [database on-line]. Provo, UT, USA: Ancestry.com Operations, Inc.,2006
Evelyn	Payne	1920 U.S. Federal Census [database on-line]. Provo, UT, USA: Ancestry.com Operations, Inc.,2010
Howard	Reid	1930 U.S. Federal Census [database on-line]. Provo, UT, USA: Ancestry.com Operations, Inc.,2002

Census citations

Maude	Roach	1930 U.S. Federal Census [database on-line]. Provo, UT, USA: Ancestry.com Operations, Inc.,2002
Arthur	Sands	1930 U.S. Federal Census [database on-line]. Provo, UT, USA: Ancestry.com Operations, Inc.,2002
Charlotte	Snyder	1910 U.S. Federal Census [database on-line]. Provo, UT, USA: Ancestry.com Operations, Inc.,2006
Charlotte	Snyder	1920 U.S. Federal Census [database on-line]. Provo, UT, USA: Ancestry.com Operations, Inc.,2010
Julia	Snyder	1870 U.S. Federal Census [database on-line]. Provo, UT, USA: Ancestry.com Operations, Inc.,2009
Julia	Snyder	1910 U.S. Federal Census [database on-line]. Provo, UT, USA: Ancestry.com Operations, Inc.,2006
Simon	Snyder Jr	1880 U.S. Federal Census [database on-line]. Provo, UT, USA: Ancestry.com Operations, Inc.,2010
Simon	Snyder Jr	1910 U.S. Federal Census [database on-line]. Provo, UT, USA: Ancestry.com Operations, Inc.,2006
Simon	Snyder Sr	1860 U.S. Federal Census [database on-line]. Provo, UT, USA: Ancestry.com Operations, Inc.,2009
Andrew	Tarr	1850 U.S. Federal Census [database on-line]. Provo, UT, USA: Ancestry.com Operations, Inc.,2009
John	Tarr	1850 U.S. Federal Census [database on-line]. Provo, UT, USA: Ancestry.com Operations, Inc.,2009

Documents

School Records					
Clarence Augustus	Brooks [II]	Diploma	Catwissa High School, 1899		
Mary Estelle	Brooks	Diploma	Coughlin High School, 1937		

Birth Certificates, Death Certificates and Cemetery Records

First Name	Last Name	Document	Issuer	Date Filed	File Number
Mary	Britton	Death Certificate	PA: Department of Health: Bureau of Vital Statistics	5/31/1913	49653
Mary Estelle	Brooks	Birth Certificate	PA: Department of Health: Bureau of Vital Statistics	8/16/1918	2130-R
Clarence Augustus	Brooks [I]	Cemetery Record	Greenwood Cemetery Grave List, Catawissa, PA	Undated	N/A
[Clarence] Augustus	Brooks [II]	Death Certificate	Connecticut State Department of Health	11/22/1942	1194
George	Brooks	Cemetery Record	Greenwood Cemetery Grave List, Catawissa, PA	Undated	N/A
William	Davies	Death Certificate	PA: Department of Health: Bureau of Vital Statistics	2/27/1956	13118
Stella Mae	Gardner	Death Certificate	CT State Department of Health	1/20/1945	1012
Henry	Jones	Death Record	Ancestry.com. Pennsylvania, Church and Town Records, 1808-1985 [database on-line]. Provo, UT, USA: Ancestry.com Operations, Inc., 2011		

Documents

Irene	James	Death Record	Greenwood Cemetery Grave List, Catawissa, PA	Undated	N/A
Harriet	Parks	Death Certificate	PA: Department of Health: Bureau of Vital Statistics	October 11. 1940	Missing
Mary	Paul	Death Certificate	PA: Department of Health: Bureau of Vital Statistics	2/25/1956	13118
Charles Albert	Paul	Death Certificate	PA: Department of Health: Bureau of Vital Statistics	7/10/1953	60728
Luther William	Snyder	Birth Certificate	PA: Department of Health: Bureau of Vital Statistics	2/14/1911	300503
Charlotte	Snyder	Death Certificate	PA: Department of Health: Bureau of Vital Statistics	6/16/1930	721
Luther William	Snyder	Death Certificate	Conn. State Department Of Health	4/3/1973	
Maude	Snyder	Death Certificate	PA: Department of Health: Bureau of Vital Statistics	2/16/1945	204
Marriage Records					
Augustus Brooks and Mary M Jones		Marriage	Ancestry.com. Pennsylvania, Church and Town Records, 1808-1985 [database on-line]. Provo, UT, USA: Ancestry.com Operations, Inc., 2011		
Clarence Brooks and Miss Stella Paul		Marriage certificate	Clerk of the Orphan's Court of Lackawanna County Pennsylvania		Numbered 2261, 1937
Samuel Gardner and Stella Mae Brooks		Marriage License	Conn. State Department Of Health (Town of New Haven)	8/11/1943	N/A
Luther William Snyder and Mary Estelle Brooks		Marriage Registration	The City of New York: Office of the City Clerk	1/30/1941	1072

Edwards Brothers Malloy
Thorofare, NJ USA
March 1, 2016